The Journey of a Dream

"All Things are Possible to those whom Believe"

Brian Andrew Tunstall

Journey of a Dream. Copyright @ 2021 by Brian Andrew Tunstall. All rights reserved. Printed in t he United State of America. No part of t his book may be used or reproduced i n any manner whatsoever without written permission. Except i n case of brief quotations embodied i n critical articles and reviews.

For more i nformation; b aunlimited@msn.com.

First Edition.
ISBN _____

Brian Andrew Tunstall
With DeeDee McNiel

Forwarded by Tanya Hart

Dedication

To every person who dares to dream and pursue your life with passion and curiosity, always believe in yourself and live a life with purpose. I wish you a life full of peace, love, laughter, and joy. May your journey be well traveled.

Acknowledgements

I am truly blessed and grateful for all the love I received from my family and friends.

My Beloved Children who have enriched my life beyond measure. "My heart is always full and overflowing with thanks to God for you as I constantly remember you in my Prayers". Ephesians 1:16

Thank you for being a part of my journey and allowing me to be a part of yours.

Table of Contents

Acknowledgements .... *iv*
Introduction .... *vii*
Forward .... *ix*
Chapter:
    "Humble Beginnings" *1*
    "The Pride of Me" *6*
    "Birth of a Dream" *17*
    "Hair Me!" *22*
    "Be Ready!" *30*
    "California Here I Come" *43*
    "Game Changer" *46*
    "Full Circle" *52*
    "Surreal Joy" *59*
    "Credentials in Hand" *62*
    "Epiphany" *76*
    "Just Can't Catch a Break" *81*
    "Yet Again" *88*
    "Not Giving Up" *94*
    "Times are Changing" *96*
    "Facing the Inevitable" *103*
    "OPEN DOORS" *105*

Introduction

The Journey of a Dream came to mind as a desire to share my life story. Looking forward, through the lens of my fears and the endless challenges, because of my determination to never give up on my dreams, I succeeded. Regardless of the barriers, naysayers and obstacles that sometimes brought me to my knees; at times, even swallowed me up in despair and had me balled into a fetal position, I survived.

Ultimately, what didn't kill me made me stronger. Success can feel like the best revenge, after you break through all the fears that once held you back. Because, to achieve anything meaningful, you must put the work in. You must push through those limiting obstacles. I have learned invaluable lessons, that have made me reach deeper inside myself. Now, I embrace a better understanding of life, love, goals, and people. Transformative and meaningful moments unfolded and rewarded me along my journey. Today, I'm still standing, persevering, and dreaming!

I hope this book will inspire and encourage the reader to believe in their dreams, live a passionate life and never give up!

"Because you have so little faith, truly I tell you, if you have faith like a grain of mustard seed, you can say to this mountain, 'Move from here to there,' and it will move. Nothing will be impossible for you."

-Matthew 17:20

Forward

Some people call me an industry veteran. I guess 50 plus years in the business is deserving of this title. My broadcast career started when I was a student at Michigan State University. It was April 4, 1968, when Martin Luther King Jr. was assassinated. I went to the University radio station the 50,000 Watt WKAR-FM and told them to put me and my two friends on the air to stop what was about to become a huge riot on campus. To our surprise they did, and the rest is history. I knew that I was destined to tell stories about African Americans and our history of building this nation. It was this passion that brought me to Los Angeles in 1990 to build BET's first Hollywood studio at the request of BET co-founder Bob Johnson. It was an exciting time in the U.S. and in my life. My colleague Brian Clarke whom I had worked with in Boston suggested we hire Brian Andrews to run the studio hair and make-up department. After interviewing several stylists, it was clear Brian was the one. He had all the right stuff, confidence, not star stuck, a great personality, and yes, he could do some fierce hair on women or men!! After Brian joined the BET team, we began to get all the big names coming to the studio and Brian always made sure that everyone looked their best when they stepped into the hot seat for our interviews. I am so proud that our BET shows gave Brian the tools to compete in an industry that didn't consider Black people important. Brian Andrews used this opportunity to become a game changer taking on the unions, and opening doors in Television and Film for other African Americans just as I had done for him. He has five Emmy nominations and is part of the Oscar- winning team on, "The Grinch Who Stole Christmas", he is an award- winning Hairstylist, Master Barber, Educator, Consultant, Certified Life Coach, and Author. He is a Screen Actor's Guild Award Winner for Hair Design and a recipient of the 2000 Hollywood Make-up Artist and Hairstylist Guild Award. But all these accolades aren't the reason you should read this book. The reason to dive into "Journey of a Dream" is to give you some insight on how to become successful against all odds. Brian Andrews has done just that, and his journey continues.

Tanya Hart
Los Angeles
September 2021

CHAPTER ONE
"Humble Beginnings"

The Journey begins...Where do I start? A little place called, Providence in Rhode Island, one of the original 13 colonies. The smallest state in the Union, but you have no idea of the power, prestige, and historical value that it has until you read my story. As I chronicle my life through my triumphs and failures, successes, and prideful moments, I'm grateful I kept moving forward and kept believing in myself at times when I wanted to give-up.

Coming from a single parent household wasn't easy. My father, Luke Tunstall II, was with us for the first three years of my life. At that time, we lived in the Hartford Housing Projects; me, my dad, my mother, Esther P. Tunstall, and my older brother, Luke Tunstall III. Sadly, my mother and father parted ways and we moved to Potters Avenue on the West End of Providence. There, we relocated into a three-family house. Me, my brother, and mother lived on the first floor, my grandmother and grandfather lived on the second floor and my aunt and uncle occupied the third floor. Even though I was surrounded by my mother's family, I was conflicted at an early age, because of not having a father present in my life and being raised by a mother. It wasn't until I was a grown man that I realized how detrimental those two factors could be. I was an energetic little boy with a mind of my own. I recall being a highly active kid who loved playing outdoors. I was involved in many activities such as the Cub Scouts and later the Boy Scouts. I loved sports; swimming in the community pool and playing community football. At a young age, I had an entrepreneurial spirit. I was a paperboy. I shoveled snow in the winter and raked leaves in the fall. I always had hustle. I took out trash for the elderly. It's a tremendous challenge for a child to grow up, having to navigate your place in the world without the guidance and love of your father. Still, I kept active and busy, but there was a void in my soul as a young boy. I don't recall my father being present in my life. Remember, I was three when my parents broke up. I don't recall ever getting a hug from my father. My brother and I never received a simple phrase from him like, "I'm proud of you, son." Unfortunately, that emotional pain was carried into my adulthood. I recall, President Barack Obama talked about the "hole" in his heart left by the absence of his father. In February of 2014, our former president launched an organization called, 'My Brother's Keeper,' to address the gaps in the lives of young men of color. It was a necessary and positive initiative to help young men of color reach their potential through mentoring and educational programs. I was a living example of a single parent youth who needed that type of support.

 Thankfully, I did have my maternal grandfather. He was a blessing in my life. I do recall many special moments with my grandfather, Edward Emanual Smith. I called him 'Pop,' but he was also known as, "Red." My grandfather was a man's-man type of a guy. He was medium tall and had a strong, thick body.

He was very, very fair. He could almost pass for an Italian white man. It was hard to tell what nationality he was. He had those light-colored, greenish-gray eyes. His hair was silky, thick, and wavy. I think it gave him great pleasure to take me under his wing and teach me how to be a man. We connected through long talks and walks. He taught me to fish and to hunt. We used to cast our fishing lines into the Twin River, and he would share words of wisdom with me. To this day, because of all those great experiences, I have an appreciation for the great outdoors.

One of the stories he shared was when he lived in Virginia. He said he grew up living between the Hatfield's and the McCoy's. The Smith family was the only black family that lived in 2between those historic Hatfield and McCoy neighbors. Pop taught me to look a man in his eyes when you talk to him. My grandfather said, you shake another man's hand with a firm handshake and your word is your bond. He lived a fascinating life and his storytelling always had me looking forward to our next time together. Pop told me he was a member of the Negro League Baseball teams; first the Brooklyn Eagles, when he lived in New York and later, when he established the Providence Eagles. Pop said he taught Satchel Paige to pitch. My beloved grandfather said he played with the Negro National League until he hurt his shoulder. Surprisingly, Pop had no formal education. He didn't read and write until very late in life. That's when he was taught by his kids. But he was always an entrepreneur and a self-employed man if I knew him. He always had his own businesses. Initially, he told me he was one of the first blacks to have a business with the Long Shoreman of New York. That man profited by his own ingenuity. My Grandfather was awe-inspiring, but he did suffer a bad stroke of luck, that became a great lesson learned. He told me he lost his first business. It was a small oversight with a big consequence. A business Contract was supposed to be for nine thousand dollars, and he signed it over for nine hundred dollars. From that loss, devastated yet still determined, he walked from New York to Providence, Rhode Island. He was penniless and homeless, but he carried on and eventually got back onto his feet. Pop took pride at being independent and self-employed. He started many businesses. For one, he made a living hauling coal. Another was cleaning out fireplaces. Pop had a wood yard business, an ice business, a pig farm (cleaning hogs and pig pens). None of his children wanted to be a part of that business! And, for a while he owned a diner. He owned a fish business, where he would take a school bus and go into the neighborhood and sell his food to the less fortunate. He had a vegetable stand. Oh, he was quite resourceful. I'm sure some of that entrepreneurial charm rubbed off on me.

    He always had a heart to feed the homeless. Pop was a kind man. He married my grandmother and they had four children. He founded, managed, and coached his own National Black League team, the Providence Eagles, pictured below.

Plus, my grandfather had swag! He was very well-known in his neighborhood. Do you remember that movie, Cotton Club? Well, there's a scene in that movie where a baseball player makes an appearance, and his name was Red. He comes in the club, looking good and greeting everyone, and that was really an emulation of my grandfather. He used to reminisce, telling me about knowing everybody back in those Cotton Club days. I remember him sharing stories about the Savoy and the Cotton Club. Pop said he hung-out with cats like Count Basie, Duke Ellington, and that's how my Aunt Elaine ended up singing with Duke Ellington at fourteen-years old. His daughter, my Aunt Elaine, was a popular jazz singer around RhodeIsland and beyond.

Pop helped me a lot. But as my adolescent years dawned, I was still missing my father and searching for self-identity. I was also dealing with mis-placed anger. I had a deep longing for love and acceptance. All too often my mother and her family disparaged my father in front of me and my brother. As we grew older, from young children to adolescence, we heard them say *he didn't amount to nothin'* and them accused us of being just like him. If you hear *"You ain't going to be nothin' just like your daddy,"* enough times you might start to believe it. But something inside of me rebelled against those toxic accusations. I told myself, you are somebody and you're going to be successful. Something inside of me was determined to prove the naysayers wrong!

CHAPTER TWO
"The Pride of Me"

My mother's side of the family is from an African-American, middle-class stature and most of them always lived in a nice house with respectable surroundings. My father's side of the family lived in a lesser desirable neighborhood. Certain neighborhoods were deemed at the top of the food chain and others, not so much. My dad came from a family of fifteen brothers and sisters. My mother's people were more college educated. On the other hand, my father's family were more blue-collar worker types. My paternal grandfather died at a young age. Consequently, my father had to drop out of high school to help support his many brothers and sisters. When I was born, my mother and father were financially challenged and lived in the Projects; a place where lower income people were housed. I don't think my mother's side of the family ever approved of that lifestyle. Without fail, each family gathering was a natural progression into a conversation that would inevitably bring up my father's name. He would often become the brunt of amusement in their conversation and ridiculed without just cause. They never had anything good to say about my dad.

There was always a derogatory word attached to his name. *"That man was never worth anything,"* they would say. *"He's never going to amount to nothing!"* were the hurtful words me and my brother heard around the dinner table. At times, we also were disparaged and accused of being just like him. People! Stop comparing your fatherless sons to their fathers! These unkind words were a negative, humiliating slap across my self-esteem. My mother's people tried to diminish me by destroying my father before my eyes. Why couldn't they se2e that? At the time, I could not make my own judgeme2nt about the man, because I did not see my father for the first fifteen years of my life. I would discover more about that separation many years later.

Meanwhile, my mother did her best with recruiting male influences into my life that she hoped would help me become a productive, young man. She looked to teachers, coaches, the community and sometimes a boyfriend or two. Unfortunately, in my mind, none of them could replace my dad.

My mother, Esther P. Tunstall, (also affectionately known as E.P.T), was quite a character! She was like Tyler Perry's comical film character, Madea, a big momma type woman and soul singer Betty Wright, all rolled into one. Esther was about five foot seven, charismatic and God had painted her a beautiful, light, caramel-brown color. I took my light skin-coloring from my mom. Although she was a big-boned woman, my mother knew how to turn a few heads. She did not have any problem getting a man. Full of confidence, she would stand in front of the mirror and sing, *"Oh – You beautiful doll, you great big, beautiful doll."*

Like everyone in our immediate family, my mother was a hardworking woman. For a while, she worked for Senator

Claiborne de Borda Pell, who represented Rhode Island from 1961 to 1997. While working for the Senator, she graduated from Nursing School. Soon after graduation, she landed a job at Providence Health Center and remained there for twenty-five plus years. My mother was not only a nurse, but quite artistic and known for her arts and crafts. She had a sweet habit of giving her dazzling crochet work to friends and family. Esther P. Tunstall crocheted everything from blankets to socks and infant wear. My mother was highly skilled, determined, methodical and super-fast. She amazed me at how many things she could acc2omplish and did each one exceptionally well. At times, she held a second job. E.P.T worked for 'Check the Florist,' part-time, assembling hundreds of ribbons weekly for the flower shop floral arrangements. She exuded the confidence of a lion but wouldn't harm a cub. She was an Eastern Star. She was a sister-friend and provided advice and support to many of the neighborhood women who needed it. My mother was outspoken and opinionated, but most people appreciated her caring advice.

E.P.T had the ability to take a broke-down man, clean him up, fix his teeth, show the man how to dress and get him looking debonair. I watched those men come home, after a hard week's work, and bring her their check. I saw my mom's boyfriend sign the check over to her and Esther P. would tuck the gift into her bosom, hand him some cash and then lay out his clothes on the bed. She would place a clean Banlon sweater on top of the bedspread next to freshly pressed slacks and put his polished shoes on the floor beneath the outfit. With a smile and a kiss, she would send him off to hang-out with the boys or go clubbing. But if he weren't home at a decent hour, for whatever reason, she'd call me and my brother to give him what she called, the 'Glad Bag Treatment.' We would pull his stuff out of the dresser drawers and stuff his things into plastic garbage bags. In a matter of minutes, we would have those bags packed and set out on the front porch. When the unsuspecting man finally did arrive home, he would know it was time to relocate. If he didn't, my grandfather would be coming down those stairs with a shotgun.

Oh, my mother was no joke. Like my grandfather, she said what she meant and meant what she said. She taught my brother and me to be respectful and independent. We learned by example, and we were trained early on how to take care of ourselves. E.P.T and my grandmother taught us how to cook, clean, sew, iron, vacuum and keep a clean house. Later, I would learn we could do that better than the average woman. E.P.T. kept us dressed impeccably. She kept a solid roof over our head, food on the table and provided us with a sense of security. My mother was my biggest cheerleader! No matter what I wanted to do, or for that matter, what I did, she supported me. If I was a male stripper, a hairdresser, or a model, there was no judgment.

Esther P. only offered loving support. She wasn't just my mom; she was mybest friend.

Our family was deeply religious. My mother, like my maternal grandmother, was born and raised in Judaism. In fact, my dad was raised that way also and my grandmothers on both sides of my family were raised in Judaism. As far as I know, even my great-grandparents were raised in the temple. We belonged to The Church of God and Saints of Christ. That was a Black Hebrew Israelite religious group, established by William Saunders Crowdy way back in 1896. The organization grew so fast and spread into so many cities of the United States that they eventually sent church leaders to six African countries, then to Cuba and even to the West Indies. Our religion teaches us that among the descendants of the original Israelites were people of color with African roots. Although it contains the word Christ in its title, the membership believes that Jesus was neither God nor the son of God. Instead, we believe he was a prophet sent by God, much the way that Jewish people believe. Our Church of God and Saints of Christ draws their beliefs from both the Old Testament of the Bible and the New Testament. We believe in wearing yarmulkas (pronounced Yakamas) and, as a young, schoolboy, I was teased a lot for wearing that small cap on my head.

I was pretty much raised by my mother, my grandmother, and my aunt Elaine. My maternal grandmother, I called her Nanny, is one of 21 siblings. Yes, my great grandmother had twenty-one children. Hers is one of the largest families in Rhode Island; the Venter-Pricefamily.

My grandmother and my mother share the same first name, Esther. Nanny was a wonderful, nurturing woman, a musical genius. She had a golden voice and perfect pitch. One of her pinnacle achievements was the time she sang with Mahalia Jackson at Carnegie Hall. She was part of a religious group called the Echoes of Melody Choir.

To reiterate, Nanny too was born into Judaism and raised my mother accordingly. Esther Venter-Price, my Nanny, was dedicated to rearing her children, homemaking and maintaining her Judaism faith. I recall my grandmother faithfully taking me on the weekends to the temple to observe and keep the Sabbath. A god fearing, bible-toting-woman, she was prominent in her community. Nanny loved God, family, and her fellow man. She believed all things are possible if you believe in the Lord.

However, she was often quick to play down my dreams. That is why I struggled with my grandmother from time to time. For some unknown reason, Nanny believed I dreamt too big. Perhaps she feared I would eventually be disappointed and fall flat on my face. In the same breath, she was also my fervent protector. I knew she loved me. I think my grandmother was just afraid I would fail or maybe she thought my dreams were not big enough. After all, her children were professional successes, and her brothers and sisters were all well-established and highly educated. One of my uncles was the first black oil man, investing in the oil business. One of her other brothers had his own landscaping company. All my aunts and uncles went to college or University, becoming secretaries, educators, nurses, and doctors. They were very collegiate people. Some of my uncles were Masons and my aunts, along with my mother, were Eastern Stars. The Order of the Eastern Star is an extension of the Masonic body. That order is based on teachings from the Bible but is open to people of all religious beliefs. There are approximately 10,000 chapters today in over twenty countries and half a million members make up the Eastern Star.

Because Nanny's children, brothers and sisters were from academia, I guess she wanted me to pursue that university path. However, my first dream was to be a singer.

As a small boy, I believed I had a good voice and I wanted to pursue dreams of becoming a recording artist and popular singer. Nanny would say, *"boy, you can't carry a tune."*

Maybe she was trying to protect my heart, but that criticism hurt my feelings and dashed my dream. Afterall, she was a gospel singer whose opinion I greatly respected. I think she insulted me because she did not want to see me become a secular singer. Being from the era of Billie Holliday and Ma Rainey, she had witnessed their wild ways and both popular artists were known for indulging in alcohol anddrugs. I suppose Nanny was being over-protective.

One evening, on December 21, 1969, I was watching Sammy Davis Jr. on the Ed Sullivan Show and I was enchanted by this multi-talented, black entertainer. I sat there, wide-eyed. I loved his sense of style and charismatic showmanship. I was really astounded when I heard everyone buzzing about him studying Judaism. They said he was being teased about his religious choice to become Jewish and I could relate. Back then, blacks were not recognized for Judaism. So, that made me even more curious about him. Like Sammy Davis Jr., I too had grappled with my Jewish identity. So, Mr. Davis stood out as a real, relatable super-star to me. Although he was a proselyte and I was born into my religion, Sammy Davis Jr. impressed me. He was a proud, black man who could not only dance, sing and act, he was a black Hebrew just like me.

I know my grandmother had good intentions, but she caused my daydream of becoming the next Sammy Davis Jr. to fade away like Rhode Island storm clouds after the rain. Her constant criticism caused my dreams of singing to evaporate.

My late Uncle Edward Emanuel Smith Jr., (we all called him Uncle Mike) was a wisdom warrior. Like my grandmother, he believed education was the key to success. Uncle Mike was an educator and always had a word of advice for anyone who would listen. He believed in being your best self and he was the first African American School Superintendent in Providence, Rhode Island. Uncle Mike was also a Professor at Rhode Island College and often lectured at Brown University. He was co-creator of the Upward Bound Program. Mike was fluent in seven languages. He wore a toupee and sang with a string quartet. He also sang opera. Oh, my Uncle Mike was a flamboyant character, very fair skinned and exhibited slightly effeminate characteristics. Culturally learned and well-traveled, the world was Uncle Mike's oyster. He developed an impressive portfolio of accomplishments and started investing in income properties at a young age. In fact, it was Uncle Mike who bought us the three-family house we lived in. After my parents broke up, it was Mike who moved my mother into the first floor of that house he purchased. He put his parents into the second floor living space and my aunt and uncle took the third floor. Uncle Mike helped develop the Time Share Program and owned properties in Florida, Rhode Island, and Hawaii. He was proud of teaching History at Classical High School in Providence. He was a dedicated educator, but my uncle also found time to sing with a local barbershop quartet. Uncle Mike was a personal advisor and friend of then Mayor Buddy Cianci, of Providence, Rhode Island. Additionally,

Mike was into astrology, palm reading, fitness, and health. I never saw him smoke or drink. He was a friendly, but private person, who loved helping others and Uncle Mike, like the rest of our family, was true tohis faith in Judaism. Like my grandmother, he too wanted me to attend a higher learning University.

Another influence on my life was my dear Uncle Ernest, a gentleman's gentleman. He was my mom's youngest brother. Uncle Ernest had a huge and infectious sense of humor. He was truly a natural born comedian. People loved Ernest. He could make you laugh at your own mother's funeral. My uncle was a smooth, classy dresser from head to toe. His fashion sense was incredible. He was the first man I ever saw get a manicure. His hands were impeccable, and he did not like to get them dirty. He was multi-faceted in his careers and could do no wrong in my grandfather's eyes. His nickname was Lucky, probably because he was a known gambler. Uncle Ernest was a pool player, a card shark, and well- known as a serious crap shooter. Uncle Ernest loved his dice. He was my Billie D. Williams role model before I met the real BillyDee Williams. The original Billy Dee, the actor, was someone I admired for his style and talent. After all, didn't he grace the covers of Jet and Ebony Magazines? At the time, those were our biggest African American publications. I became a big fan after seeing Billy D. Williams act in the movies, *Lady Sings the Blues* and *Mahogany*. My uncle Ernest personified this handsome, smooth-talking character. Unfortunately, Ernest left us at the early age of 35-years-old, when he suffered a massive heart attack. My suave, sophisticated, well-dressed uncle made a lasting impression on my life.

Aunt Elaine, aka Star Child, was consistently my prayer-warrior. She is my godmother and my ride-or-die aunt. I call her aunt 'Laine and she personifies the highest level of loyalty you could ever find in one person. My Aunt 'Laine always exposed me to what I now refer to as "the dream." Early in my life, she was a Jazz, R&B and Gospel singer. She originally sang with the Duke Ellington Band at the tender age of fourteen-years old. A very vital part of my fashion and styling sense came from both Uncle Ernest and Aunt 'Laine. She oozed class and has always been fashion forward. All the men in Rhode Island seemed to fancy Aunt 'Laine. Class is something you cannot buy, and she was born with an abundance of it. She's the kind of woman who could dine with the Queen of England and then, go down to the local bar and have a few drinks with the boys, but still be a lady. Between you-and-me, my aunt could throw a mean right hook. There are stories that aunt 'Laine has-been known to crack open a head or two with a blackjack or cut some unsuspecting soul with a straight razor if that person got out of line or threatened to harm her or her beloved family.

One thing I will always remember is how she exposed my brother and me to the entertainment world. At an early age, aunt 'Laine introduced us to people like comedian Mom's Mabley, R&B singer and drummer, Jefferey Osborne, and a gospel and R&B recording artist called, lots a Poppa to name a few. She sang with the R&B Jazz Group Elaine Smith and the Emanon; (no name, spelled backwards). My brother and me tagged along to some of her gigs, her rehearsals and even jam sessions. I remember one club called Pios. It had Go-Go Cages hanging from the ceiling. Boy, did my brother and I love to play in those cages.

Aunt 'Laine always kept me on track. She is a force of light and she's a never wavering prayer-warrior who consistently encouraged my dreams. Even today, she is quick to lead me and our family in a beautiful scripture we favored. Over the years, it has become our family prayer. *"Our Father, who art in Heaven, hallowed be thy name."*

never end a conversation with my aunt 'Laine without saying, I love you very much. Peace be unto thee. Like I said, aunt 'Laine dragged me and my brother around to concerts and to her gigs, opening our eyes to a different lifestyle and to the entertainment world from a backstage seat. I must admit, me and my brother, Luke Tunstall III, who I fondly call, Junie, were more than a handful. We were thick-as-thieves and a very mischievous duo. We were glued to the hip brothers and best friends. Our laughter roared, snapped, crackled, and popped through our neighborhood like fireworks. Everything, and anything was funny. Oh, we were so silly. My brother had my mother's warm, caramel complexion, a disarming smile, and a great sense of humor. Junie adds to my Mantra, *"I got to be me."* For sure, he epitomizes that saying. My brother is going to do everything his way. He is stubborn, thick-headed, and free-spirited, period! I found myself being envious of his *"blow in the wind"* mentality. While I was busy planning and worrying, my brother Junie was quick to tell me, "Don't *sweat the small stuff, bro."* My whole life, my big brother was my fierce protector. We laughed and cried together; shared our secrets and planned our dreams. I was determined to include my brother as part of my own big dream. By the time we both attended vocational High School, we had each chosen to take Barber classes. That's when we began planning to own a chain of Barber Shops together. We chose the name *'Brothers.'* The seed was planted when we were still young teens. At that point, the future remained a distant star on my soon-to-be successful horizon.

CHAPTER THREE
"Birth of a Dream"

I was the more serious child and I felt a gravity of emotions when seeing my friends interacting with their fathers. It only made me more upset about my father not being present. Junie used to tell me not to worry about it, but I know it affected me brother too. During my childhood, my dad's absence was hurtful. I missed not having someone to teach me how to be a man from a male perspective. The childhood friends, who used to hang-out at my house, rarely invited me to their homes. I did not know why. That was disappointing and it made me feel unaccepted and rejected. Was it the Judaism? I wondered., was it the yarmulka perched upon my head or my single-parent household? I was confused.

Then, abruptly, when I was ten years old, our family dynamics changed. My mother started dating a Caucasian man. My brother and I were shocked, because as soon as he showed up, we started going to a Catholic school. Mom's new friend was convinced it would be better for us. Suddenly, because he was Catholic, he felt that private school would provide better opportunities for my brother and me.

Now, I was faced with yet another confusing and emotionally weird adjustment. As soon as we were enrolled, I started hearing whispers from the priest and the nuns, commenting on why this little black boy comes to Catholic school wearing a yarmulka? The sting of embarrassment was too m2uch. Back then, only Popes and high priests wore yarmulkas, I was informed by the disapproving staff.

After that first day at the private Catholic school, I begged my mother not to send me back. For one, there were no children of color, and all my friends were at my former public school. Not to mention, I heard the whispered comments of the nuns behind my back. But it was to no avail. E.P.T. ignored my complaints. I was really depressed about the Catho2lic school situation and then, something unexpected happened.

The evening of December 14, 1969, Aunt Elaine had to plead with my mother to let us stay up late and watch this episode of the Ed Sullivan Show. She orchestrated watching the show, because she felt that it was an important, historic moment for my brother and me to witness. This was the first-time performance of the Jackson 5 group on a major, syndicated television program. She explained, they were the new, Motown teen sensation. We crowded around the television. Show-time! The Jackson 5 appeared, and the young boy's group sang, a Sly and the Family Stone song called, "Stand." Their performance included several dance numbers, and they were full of excitement and energy! I will never forget, the youngest brother, Michael, was wearing a large, brim hat and vest. He told this story about a girl he met in the sandbox at school. His monologue led up to the Smokey Robinson hit record, "Who's Loving You." Needless to say, I was completely star-struck by eleven-year- old Michael's, talent, and style. The third song was off-the-chart. It was their first single "I Want You Back." I was amazed and dazzled by their performance. Michael was around my age, yet so poised, confident, and mature. He had an incredibly soulful voice and impressive dance moves. What an enormous talent! That evening, I immediately became a huge fan. Since he was the youngest and closer to my age than his brothers, I found him more relatable. In that moment, I reclaimed my dream of singing and hoped that I too could achieve greatness as an entertainer.

After watching that Ed Sullivan show, I was extremely excited and pumped up! I ran to my room and pulled out the biggest brim hat and the most fashionable vest I owned. I spent the next hour or so impersonating James Brown's dance moves. This went on for weeks, leading up to having the courage to participate in a local Talent Show. I secretly entered under the name, Brian Andrew, purposely leaving out my Tunstall surname. You see, my uncle ran the Summer Program and I did not want any perceived favoritism to overshadow my experience. Plus, I didn't want my family to rain on my parade.

That fateful afternoon, I was ready and looking good in my steel-blue suit, pressed white, cotton shirt and with every hair in place. I was planning to impersonate Smokey Robinson's cool style. My mother and grandmother were obviously surprised when I walked out of the bedroom dressed to perform. The two women exchanged looks.

"Why are you dressed in a suit?" my grandmother wanted to know.

I just smiled and said, *"You'll see."*

When they called the Brian Andrew name, I paused for a moment. Then, as I headed for the stage, my mother and grandmother realized that Brian Andrew name belonged to me. I leapt into the spotlight with confidence and loudly, told the crowd, *"C'mon. Clap your hands!"* My enthusiasm was contagious, and I convinced people to participate.

Using my young man, tenor voice, sounding a tiny bit like Smokey Robinson, I began to sing, "OH Happy Day."

It was a proud moment for my mother, Grandmother, and my uncle Mike. With the audience captivated and in the palm of my hand, the whole family began cheering me on! I think my grandmother may have had second thoughts about my vocal gift.

After much begging and pleading, that following fall school year, I left the private Catholic school and attended Gilbert Stuart Middle School. I participated in a music class, sang in the school band, and joined a theatrical class. I even played Aladdin in the school play. I became President of the Student Council, raised an unprecedented amount of money for Guatemala after the 1976 earthquake and appointed my brother as Vice President of the Student Council. At last, my brother and I were back around our people and our neighborhood friends. Our family bond of brotherhood was stronger than ever. I never wanted to leave Junie behind. I am my Brother's Keeper, and he is mine! Even at that young age, I was still dreaming about us having our own company and being partners.

Middle school was a great time in my life. I began to feel incredibly good about myself. I was more outgoing, and my life took a decisive turn as I made friends and discovered girls.

CHAPTER FOUR
"Hair Me!"

Our weekly Saturday ritual was, my mother would take my brother and I to get our hair cut at Dottie's Barber shop. Afterwards, she would drag us to Arthur's Beauty Salon to get her hair done. Although, I was young, something in my spirit didn't sit well at Arthur's beauty shop. I was a precocious and inquisitive, young boy. Consequently, I was always peppering everybody with a lot of questions. For example, I wanted to know why the salon was named Arthur's when Candie was the owner? Candie was also my mother's hairstylist. She was a pretty lady with a low, silky voice and an hourglass figure. All her movements were graceful, like a dancer, and sometimes they seemed exaggerated. Me, being the nosy one in my family, began speculating. I had my suspicions, once I got up close to Candie and noticed this pretty lady had whiskers protruding through her makeup. Back at home, my brother and I talked about it in whispers. I told him I really didn't like going to the Salon. I was uncomfortable! Plus, in the neighborhood, I had heard rumors about this beauty salon. People said the Owner was a Man. What? Candie is a dude? So, the next time our mother dragged us down to that salon, I took a closer look. I observed Candie with the beautiful figure, but she also had masculine hands and oversized feet stuffed into her shoes. My suspicions were confirmed. When leaving the Salon, I was always a gentleman and made sure my mother was safe in the car first. I opened her door and stood there until she settled in. Then, I walked around and got into the car myself.

I had started feeling self-conscious about being at that beauty salon and hoped none of my friends saw me leaving the place. In those days, the LGBTQ community was not as acceptable as it is today. As a truth-seeker 2and a very inexperienced youth, it was only a matter of time before I asked my mother if Candie was a man? Seated in the frontseat of our car that afternoon, I posed the question.

The slap happened so quickly; I didn't even see it coming. The sting left my light-skinned face red and throbbing. My palm shot up to my burning cheek and I could hear my brother snickering in the back seat of our car. I was only seeking the truth, which, I learned, often comes with a price and a consequence.

The following Saturday, much to my discomfort, my mother shared our little episode with her hairdresser, Candie, and made me apologize to her. She graciously accepted my apology and didn't treat me any differently. I thought she might have gotten angry or given me the silent treatment. But no, Ms. Candie remained the same, treating me kindly and making me feel like part of her extended family. Overtime, I became more comfortable at the salon. I even started my own little hustle, offering to help Candie by sweeping up the floor and passing the end papers and hair rollers to her. In exchange, she offered me a little cash, which I quickly stuffed into my empty pants pocket. Besides, working in the salon made the time pass quickly. My brother and I couldn't wait to go home and play with our friends. Just sitting around drove me crazy! I would rather be busy, so I channeled my energy into helping.

Another thing I learned at the beauty salon was Sex Education 101. The clientele of sexy ladies chattered constantly. Their nasty, man-talk and explicit stories excited my curiosity. Trust and believe, I took notes. Later, down the road, it helped me with my lady friends. I chatted away with those talkative ladies, filling time at the hair salon. Some of them, I swear, were flirting with me! Damn! I was young, but not too young to start flirting right back. They used to say to my mother, *Oh, he's so cute! He's going to be a heartbreaker.* Little did I know how true those predictions would be.

started paying more attention to the before-and-after looks of the lady's hairdos. I watched the hairstylists cut and style wigs, half-pieces, and push their clientele's hair into those extravagant beehive hairdos that were popular at the time. Back then, Diahann Carroll was the first black woman on television starring in a weekly series. It was a popular show called Julia. I watched that show with an understudy's eye, paying close attention to the way Ms. Carroll styled her hair.

By the time I was twelve or thirteen, I discovered I had a real appreciation for hairstylists and barbers. I had always been interested in hair cutting and becoming a barber, but the salon environment also interested me. When I accompanied my mother, I paid strict attention to how the hairstylists performed their occupations. Many of the female customers asked me for my opinion on what hairdo they should try or after they were cut and styled, they sought my approval. These female customers made me feel good about myself. At thirteen, I became confident and comfortable with my individual swag for the first time. Perhaps those older women at Arthur's Beauty Salon helped me to see the value of an attractive man and their compliments lifted me to new heights. As a young man, I was less uptight and opinionated. By getting to know Candie and spending time at her salon, I realized she was a good person. I became less homophobic and learned a valuable lesson. Never judge a book by its cover.

My dream of singing slowly faded as I became a teenager. I was an all "A" student, a high achiever. Academically, I soared and of course my family assumed I would attend a university. I always loved sports and for a while I pursued a football career. I was active on the school football team, and I was a particularly good football player. However, I was never large in statue and size. Back then, they had height requirements and weight requirements that I just didn't meet. That stopped me from accomplishing my dream of becoming a pro football athlete.

Looking back, I recall developing an interest in cutting and styling hair as a pre-teen. I used to walk past the Woolworth's store and admire a clipper set that was displayed in their window. It was close to my birthday, when my Aunt Myrtle asked me what I wanted for a birthday present? I think I was twelve, coming up on thirteen. I said I wanted that clipper set. Well, she gifted me those shiny clippers for my birthday, but no one in the neighborhood or in my family would trust me to cut their hair.

My brother Junie had a pet poodle at that time. I decided to give my brother's dog a haircut. I wanted to clean him up, put the puffs around his paws and transform his matted hair and shaggy appearance. I grabbed my new clippers and set out to give my brother's poodle some style. Funny as that story may be, that was my first experience with doing hair. Honestly, I made that dog look so good, everybody was buzzing about the dog's haircut. A neighborhood friend of mine, his name was David Applegate, had a big round, red afro. For whatever reason, he believed in me. One day, he trusted me to give him a clipper cut. I made his bushy afro so perfectly round and so stunning that all the other neighborhood kids were impressed. These experiences encouraged me to pursue barber school.

One afternoon, I recall my Aunt Elaine walking into the house holding a blonde wig. Wigs were the hottest craze at that time. She and my mother used to go to a wig store called Dee's Golden Finger, which was a very popular wig store in Rhode Island. That's where Aunt 'Laine purchased her blonde wig. She was preparing to sing that evening. When she went to take a hot bath and prepare for her event, I kept staring at that wig. Not realizing the value or the importance of the wig, or for that matter, her event that evening, I decided the wig needed bangs! I wanted my aunt 'Laine to look like Diahann Carroll. So, I took a pair of craft-scissors and without hesitation, I started sniping away to make bangs on her expensive wig. I was full of myself and feeling highly creative as I snipped at the fake hair. I took pride in designing a hairstyle surprise for my favorite aunt. Needless to say, my Aunt Elaine was NOT happy with me.

"Bangs?" she hollered, picking up her brand-new wig and shaking it at me.

She was shocked and at first wanted to punish me. She chastised me for nearly half an hour, pacing back and forth, while clutching the blond wig in her left hand. I could hear my heart beating outside of my chest, waiting, at any given second, for the beat down I expected. Thankfully, it never came. Matter of fact, when she finally stood in front of the mirror and tried that hair piece on, Aunt 'Laine made slight adjustments and wore that wig! It looked good on her too.

My new-found success, styling her wig, gave me the confidence to be bold with my creativity. I carried myself differently. The more experienced I became, the more self-assured I was that entering a vocational school and becoming a barber was the way to go. My family protested, especially Pop, my grandfather. He thought that career was beneath me. He also thought that messing with hair was for women to do, not 'real' men.

People can be so cruel, especially when you're different from what society views as normal or what they believe is normal. My childhood pain still lies buried in my soul. I remember every mean word that was spoken against me. I endured the put-downs and hateful criticisms. I had to ignore my family accusing me of not living up to what others expected of me. It hurt! But I was relentless in my career pursuit. What was wrong with me pu2rsuing a barber career? In my teenaged mind, I was going to show those people that I would make it. I would be successful, period! Even as a young man, I knew success is not about trying to prove someone wrong. It's always about proving to yourself that you are capable, and you can achieve your dream. I knew, with every fiber of my being, that if I put my heart and soul into it and pursued my pathway to success, I would be successful. Success begins with a mindset, with an unwavering persistence. For some reason, I believed there was absolutely nothing I couldn't achieve.

I decided not to attend Classical High School, because my passion was to pursue becoming a barber. A Vocational

Program at Central High School suited me perfectly because they offered barber training. Sadly, my decision completely disappointed and infuriated my family. Specifically, my well-traveled, educated, seven-language-speaking Uncle Mike. He was furious! Uncle Mike thought attending Barber School was unacceptable. His comments still ring savagely in my ears. That anger he exhibited, when I told him my plans, was palpable. Experiencing his raised voice, from a man that was always soft spoken and mild mannered, really shocked me. His words cut like a sword.

"Barber?" he shouted. *"You're not going to amount to anything. You're not going to make money being a barber. Where's the success in that?"* He verbally attacked me. *"*

You should attend Classical High School and be something. You're an all "A" student. You could win a scholarship to college. You could easily become a Lawyer or a Doctor," he continued his tirade.

Of course, bringing up my father at this point of the conversation was predictable. *"You'll be just like your daddy and amount to nothing,"* he told me. My uncle said I would be laughed at and ridiculed.

Me, being an outspoken fourteen-year-old and confident too, responded quickly. I wasn't disrespectful to my Uncle Mike, but with pride in my voice I told him, *"I'll show you. Not only will I be successful as a barber, but I will also be recognized. I've got big plans. You'll see."*

My older brother was already enrolled in barber school at the vocational high school. I soon joined him, carefully choosing my curriculum, and feeling a sense of excitement about mastering something I loved doing. Around that same time, my favorite Aunt 'Laine suggested I try a new look for my high school debut. So, she gave me a perm. That changed my whole personality. I had this big, round afro at the time. But, after she gave me that perm, I guess I thought I was Billy Dee Williams or somebody. I don't know who I thought I was. In my teenaged mind, I felt kind of like that Vinnie Barbarino character John Travolta played in the movies. Suddenly, I had very long flowing hair. At that time, the Super Fly movie was popular in the African American community and maybe I thought I was a Super Fly kind of guy. I don't who I was trying to be. You know, Super Fly had that long, silky permed hairdo and was always dressed to kill, with several beautiful women hanging on his arm. I had a pretty active imagination, and that perm changed my entire persona.

In high school, some thought I was arrogant, cocky or conceited. I was none of those things, but I was confident! Perhaps I was misunderstood because I wore suits to school and carried a briefcase. I had the mindset of importance and becoming a successful businessman. I was confident in knowing I was going to be somebody, someday. That was confusing to many of my peers. My classmates wondered why I was getting all the ladies. Jealousy is vicious. Everyday there was some scuffling and dodging other boys and bullies over petty things. My brother, Luke, was my protector. Junie always had my back. Some days, I felt like there was a bounty on my head.

Regardless of the ups and downs and distractions, I continued to get good grades. My problem in middle school and high school was that I was considered the class clown. My school mates and teachers thought I was an attention seeker. That didn't always shine favorably on me. Fortunately, I always had my brother Junie as my back up. But then, one fateful day, my world changed drastically.

CHAPTER FIVE
"Be Ready!"

It was 1975 and a couple of guys named Bill Gates and Paul Allen had just created a company called Microsoft that made big waves in technology. After much protest, the Vietnam war finally came to an end and the former teamster boss, Jimmy Hoffa, made headlines when he disappeared without a clue. A very funny, late-night comedy show premiered on television called, "Saturday Night Live" and Minnie Ripperton's five-octave voice was singing "Loving You" on popular radio stations across the country.

I was still in high school, but I always felt like I was born ready. Some folks say, get ready. I say, be ready! Opportunities are fleeting. Luck or maybe just being in the right place at the right time can heighten your success. I was determined to be present in space and time, while making consistent steps towards accomplishing my own vivid dreams of success. But first I had to deal with a blow from my brother.

Junie started giving my mother a whole heap of trouble. He was fifteen and feeling himself. E.P.T. could no longer control my brother, so she sent him to California to live with our dad. My dream of opening "Brothers" barbershop went flying right out the window.

Down the road, my brother achieved success in his own right. Junie became an accomplished journeyman and custom metal polisher, specializing in precious metals. He did prestigious work for people such as Jay Leno. He was hired to polish Leno 's fabulous, custom car collection. He also worked on the cars in the famous movie Titanic and in Aretha Franklin's Pink Cadillac video that promoted the popular song, "Freeway of Love."

I was hurt when my brother took a different life path from mine, but I know he would give me the shirt off his back. Junie's always been the president of my fan club, for sure. We share a mutual respect in knowing, even though we took separate life paths, we're still and will always be brothers and best friends.

Pictured here is my brother "Junie" Luke Tunstall III with Jay Leno.

My brother and I had been like Siamese twins, joined at the hip. Once he left home, I started getting into all kinds of devilment, because now I'm home by myself. Suddenly, mischievous and rebellious behavior became my two best friends. I started having way too many girlfriends. I was dating one, then five or six girls at a time. I was very fashion forward. I wore crazy colors, looking like a male peacock and feeling like one too. I wasn't afraid to wear canary yellow or hot pink suits and slacks. Like the male peacock, I knew fancy feathers attracted females. Also, I was known for creating crazy hair styles. In fact, I was changing my hair all the time, from pompadours to Super Fly conks. I'd have a new hair style every week. I was almost like Prince, before there was a Prince.

Some of my classmates thought I was gay, wearing all that colorful clothing and changing my hairstyle, perhaps to the excess. So, girls would approach me to see what I would do. One thing would lead to another, and they'd quickly find out I was not gay. Then they would tell other girls about it and what we did, blah, blah, blah. The next girl would say, oh, I am going to date him. So, being sexual became a repetitive motion. Personally, I found girls my age didn't interest me. I was always attracted to older girls. When I was a freshman in high school, I was dating seniors. By the time I was a senior, I was dating college girls. Oh man, I was way ahead of myself.

Eighteen years old and my life started shaping-up and moving forward, despite my family's negative comments about my dream of pursuing a barber's career. Sure, at times it was hard to stay positive. However, my goals were meaningful to me, and I was determined. I learned to program my mind to do what it takes to push past obstacles. Staying mentally tough and applying a positive mindset, I made my plans and kept them close to my vest. That's how, I believe, I was able to eventually reach my goals.

Around this same time, my father's mother became extremely ill and passed away. At age fifteen, I finally got to briefly meet my father when he returned to Providence, Rhode Island for his mother's funeral. This brief meeting piqued my curiosity. I wanted to know more about the man who had fathered me. My brother was continuously feeding me bits and pieces about our dad. His long-distance messages boasted about how much fun Luke Tunstall was and all the things they did together. Junie told me about them going to the beach and enjoying the Pacific Ocean. He said my father had a van and he and my brother were doing all these amazing things together. So, of course I wanted to experience that closeness and camaraderie with my dad for myself. At fifteen years old, I took a bus ride to California to meet my father. My mother probably breathed a sigh of relief, because first her oldest son was raising cane and giving her all kinds of trouble, and now I too was challenging her authority and pretty much being wild and unmanageable.

To make a long story short, that's when I discovered Luke Tunstall II was nothing like what my brother had described. I stayed about 3 to 4 months. I had to go live with my aunt, because me and my father did not get along at all. I was still a kid, trying to be grown. He was intent on being my father and telling me what to do. I stayed with my aunt, who had five children. I figured taking care of one more would not bother her, so I went and stayed with Aunt Loris, my father's sister. I was supposed to be going to school but suddenly, I started getting sick. So, my aunt called my father because he was the one actually responsible for me. My father came to her house and took one look at me and said, *"What's the problem?*

I said, I don't know.

My aunt responded, *"Oh Luke, I think he's got the flu."*

My father took another look at me and said, *"He don't have the flu. He's gotten some girl pregnant."*

Well, that shocked me and Aunt Loris. My Aunt said, *"What do you mean he got someone pregnant?"*

My father spoke emphatically. *"He has morning sickness. I got morning sickness when his mother was pregnant every time. It runs in our family. The men get morning sickness when their women get pregnant."*

Well, that got my immediate attention. So, I called my sweetheart at that time, a girl who I was very much in love with and who loved me in return. At first, she denied being pregnant. I came to find out later, she wanted to make sure that she was past the three-month period, so her father wouldn't force her to have an abortion. She wanted our baby. My first child's mother is two years older than I am. I was kind of a bad boy, back then. By the time I graduated high school, I already had fathered two children by two different women.

My trip to California was cut short and I returned home to continue my barber education. Ironically, the movie "Shampoo" was released in 1975. Warren Beatty played a Beverly Hills Hairdresser. He was a handsome lady's man with a complicated life and lascivious behavior. That movie encouraged me and solidified my decision to pursue doing what I loved to do.

In my vocational high school, once you completed the first few years of your vocation, if your grades were up to par, (and I was a straight "A" student) once you had all your points in line to graduate, their system would allow you to go to school half day. It was called the Work Release Program. I attended school only in the morning. To participate in the program, a student had to take an English class, or math or science class. I had passed all of those early on. That allowed me to leave school for half day and find work at my craft. Well, I found myself a job and I moved out of my mother's house when I was sixteen years old. I was doing well enough to afford my own apartment. I was a hustler and did a lot of things to survive. Still attending high school half day, I worked at a local barber shop in the afternoon, and I picked up modeling jobs too. For a while, I even made money being a male stripper. My rent had to be paid! By the time I was seventeen, I had two children, the responsibility of father hood and career dreams to be fulfilled.

Following Graduation from High School, I attended Arthur Angelo's School of Cosmetology and Hair Design. I wrestled with my decision because I had chosen a profession that my family frowned upon. But I finally realized, a barber could make much more money doing women's hair than just cutting men's hair in a barbershop. I wanted to master hair styling too.

While attending Arthur Angelo's, I decided to enter the team hair competition. Picture me, all confident and flamboyant and I was the only black student in an all-white cosmetology school. Consequently, I faced immediate rejection. They wouldn't even invite me to be on their hair teams. Undaunted and stubborn, I entered as an Independent Stylist, formed my own team, and competed against the Arthur Angelo's school team. I can still remember walking into that huge auditorium with my few assistants. They had preparation tables available and each one was numbered. Each team was then assigned a number and we would go to that table, set up, and get ready for the show. It was like a hair fashion- show type competition, a battle of the hair dressers! Everyone brought their "A" game and came up with a theme. I had ten models. I adopted an 'around-the-world' theme. Part of my creative and unique styling radiated other countries and cultures. My company and my brand still use that world symbol today, because I never planned to be just a citizen of Rhode Island or America. I had a world view of my talent. I planned to travel worldwide and to touch continents with my work.

Well, guess what? I won that competition! Needless to say, the next time around, with embarrassment dripping from their faces, I was eagerly welcomed onto the Arthur Angelo School Hair Team.

While attending the Arthur Angelo School, I won several Stylistic Awards and earned a scholarship to the prestigious Pivot Point International. This was a special training center for hair techniques in Chicago, Illinois. In an Industry, where I remained the only black Stylist, once again I was met with the challenge of racism. I found myself having to "do more–do better – work harder, alongside my peers, who were often not as talented. Little did I know, these in-your-face, racist, and judgmental moments would only prepare me for what lay ahead.

Each accolade I accomplished was met with my hallelujah praise and more determination! Everything was coming full circle. My journey had finally defined its' directional course. I thought often of the trio of support that helped and influenced me. Dottie Magnum Thomas, Elaine Briggs, and Rhonda "Jewels" Smith. Their encouragement was extremely instrumental in helping me pursue my dreams.

Dottie-Magnum-Thomas was my Barber as a young boy. She had a smile that felt like a warm hug. Dottie always made me feel grown up in her chair, even when my feet couldn't touch the foot stool. Looking back, I admired the way she spoke to me, like I was an adult. Year after year, sitting in her barber chair, she listened to me spout my dreams and aspirations. That talented, female barber made me feel like she was genuinely interested in my plans. I doubt that she realized it meant so much to me, but as a young man and to this day, her encouraging words reverberate. She was one of the few who believed in me and propelled me towards my future success.

Elaine Briggs was one of my mother's favorite hair stylists and lifetime best friend. Ms. Briggs also believed in my dreams. We shared many memorable conversations early in my career. She would show me different hair tricks and taught me how to care for and grow hair. She radiated a beautiful and inviting spirit that glowed from the inside out. Elaine was a strong, independent, Cape Verdean women who taught me a lot about being an entrepreneur.

I was inspired by Elaine's classy establishment on the East side of Providence, Rhode Island. It had a first-class ambience and was very attractive to the eye. As a student, with dreams of being a successful entrepreneur, I thought her example of excellence was something I wanted for myself. She ran a very no-nonsense hair salon. Elaine Briggs was punctual, down to the second. She kept her place pristine and clean. When you entered her establishment, there was a nice counter at the front door. There, you would see new products, hair greases, little combs and brushes and various hair accessories. She kept an appointment book and had a friendly, well-dressed receptionist who would get the client a cup of coffee or a glass of wine while they waited. It was a very prestigious salon. Elaine Briggs showed me a completely different approach to running a hair salon as a serious, professional business.

While going to beauty school. I worked in my cousin's hair salon. Rhonda Jewels Smith also supported my dreams. She coached me and shared tips about styling wigs, hair pieces, and applying roller sets and comb-outs. Rhonda knew all the important fundamentals of becoming a great hairstylist. Her persistence and ingenuity helped me conquer my fears when it came to creating and imagining high-end hairstyles. I'm forever grateful for her teachings and her helpful instruction. She showed me how to run a successful hairdressing business. My cousin also offered not only expertise in hair salons, but also other lessons in life.

Rhonda had a high-end salon in downtown Providence. Her clientele consisted of judges, lawyers and the more elite of Rhode Island. She was styling singers, painters, and many professionals. Rhonda was doing big things in Providence at that time. See, here's the catch with my relative. My cousin was Ron, a man, and a very handsome male model. He wound up having a sex change later in life. But, when I was a young teen, my cousin was a popular male model who graced thecovers and pages of various sepia magazines.

I was innocent of the many ways of the world and Cousin Ron helped school me. I admired my cousin. He was about fifteen years older than am and wore impeccable attire. His shoes were always polished to a high shine and Ron was consistently stylish and fly. Oh, the women loved Ron. They fluttered around him like hummingbirds feasting on sugar water. One afternoon, while I was working at his popular and exclusive salon, all these fine women were throwing themselves all over my cousin. That day, when the salon business slowed down, Ron took a break, shook his head, and told me, *"These women are getting on my nerves. They make me sick to my stomach."*

I had been sitting there, admiring all the attention my handsome cousin was getting from the many gorgeous female clients and his words puzzled me. How could these gorgeous women make him sick to his stomach? That was the day Cousin Ron explained to me that he was gay. He told me that he wasn't attracted to women at all. Ron confessed that he preferred men. Shocked, I immediately flashed back to my experiences at Arthur's Salon and to my mother's hairstylist, Ms. Candie. That experience suddenly got a lot more personal when the gay man sitting before me was a member of my own family.

Ron, who later became Rhonda, was very protective of me as a young man. I was sixteen and he recognized my innocence. Ron set out to introduce me to another culture. He supported my dreams of becoming an innovative and successful hairdresser, but he didn't want his talented, little cousin taken advantage of because of ignorance. He told me, in the profession I had chosen, I would encounter many gay guys. He said I didn't have to participate in that lifestyle, but I needed to be aware of it. It was back in the disco era and Ron dragged me off to explore many underworlds gay clubs, where I saw cross-dresser parties and sex-changed men. He even took me to a place where he, himself, dressed up as a woman and danced to win a trophy prize from his gay community. It was a scene very much like the ones pictured in the Netflix series, "Pose." My cousin wanted me to understand the gay language and the gay culture. They had their own slang. They had their own codes. Ron wanted to expose me to all of that, because he knew I was pursuing a career as both a male model and hairstylist. He recognized, all too well, there was a stigma attached to both occupations.

We both knew our family didn't approve of our career paths, partly because they were homophobic. Because of their uptight fears, I found myself always trying to prove to people that I wasn't gay. Some folks assumed, just because of my flamboyant dress and desire to pursue a cosmetology career, that I was homosexual. Cousin Ron encouraged my career path, but he wanted me to be prepared for what I would run into along the way. He wanted me to be the straight man I had always been and to not be intimidated by family members or other men in our industry.

"Just be you," Cousin Ron was adamant.

It was an exciting time to be in the hair business. But, along with a movement of black pride and self-awareness came a reflection of our African roots displayed by our hairstyles. In the seventies, men chose to wear dashikis instead of shirts and women of color wore huge, colorful beaded earrings and necklaces. We were singing along with James Brown, *"say it loud. I'm black and I'm proud."* But by the 1980's, a new style and product for hair care bombarded the scene and took center stage. The curtains of my industry pulled apart to spotlight, the Jheri Curl.

This new African American, permanent-wave hairstyle was invented by Jheri Redding. The Jheri Curl gave thick, coarse hair a glossy, often greasy look, hanging in wet curls around proud, people-of-color faces. This hair treatment was personified by celebrities like Michael Jackson; rapper, Eazy E.; actor Samuel L. Jackson; R&B crooner, Rick James, the Godfather of Soul, James Brown and Eric LaSalle, an actor in the film 'Coming to America.' Oh, Jheri Curls were all the rage in the 1980s.

I made the right choice by going to beauty school and perfecting my craft. Locally, my reputation was growing around Providence, Rhode Island. The son of the founder of Cornell Enterprises, based in Woonsocket, Rhode Island, recruited me to help their company promote a new product. In co-ordination with the Abbott Company, they manufactured afro combs and picks. I recall using those big, plastic picks with the black power fist attached. But recognizing the change of direction in hair styles, the Cornell Company wanted to produce a product that did not rely on heavy chemicals like lye to straighten and style thick, textured hair. Thus, was born, The Freedom Curl.

The more organic Freedom Curl was one of the first cream-based types of Jheri Curl on the market. It contained no lye. I started off with this company as an Educational Specialist and swiftly worked my way up to National Styling Director. I used and promoted their product during my popular hairstyling shows and educated their national team on the use of their product. It was a dream fulfilled!

After graduation, my adrenaline rush was in overdrive as I balanced all the many opportunities coming my way. I was doing hair shows all over the country, as well as becoming the advertisement model for the Freedom Curl. I was pictured on the branded box for their product. I became the poster child for their popular product, and I was on billboards, on buses, magazines, everywhere. Later, I participated in the first Bronner Brothers International Beauty Show and several more, including the Big Show Expo Tour. I participated in the very first Black and Gold Trade Show in Los Angeles. That was exciting! Especially, since I was revisiting California for the second time around, at a time in my life when I was more mature and more productive. My string of successes sparkled like the gold chains around my neck. I was feeling pleased with myself and my life's direction. The palm of my hand itched for more money, more accomplishments, more growth in my business. I felt like a star running back who just caught the football and made a spectacular ninety-yard touchdown.

But, although my amazing opportunities were like a dream come true, I was still grappling with my desire to reach another level. All the exposure, knowledge, and contacts I was gaining, just whet my appetite for exciting, bigger and better achievements. Being back in Southern California, I couldn't ignore my desire to stay a little longer and give Hollywood a chance.

CHAPTER SIX

"California Here I Come"

California dreaming! With the new opportunity to travel and spend time in Southern California, I found myself intrigued by the boldness of L.A. city and energized by the Los Angeles vibe. After the Black and Gold Trade Show event, returning home to Rhode Island, was anti-climactic. I was restless. So, I took another leap of faith. On the 4th of July weekend, in 1985, I packed up everything I owned, stuffed it into my blue Datsun 280Z and headed across the country. I was fearless! I think my family and friends thought I had lost my mind.

Aunt Loris, on my father's side, was generous enough to have affordable housing lined up until I got on my feet. From that connection, I was able to begin a dialogue with my father, which meant a great deal to me. It had been a decade since we had communicated.

The 'move' was challenging! California was a serious hustle. Within three, short months, I was able to get my own apartment, obtain my California hairdresser's license and become an Instructor at the Wilfred Beauty Academy. At that time, it was one of the largest beauty schools in the country.

Simultaneously, I was getting connections and gigs styling models who were doing advertising print work. Concurrently, I was diligent in trying to work my way into Hollywood's elite television and film world. The challenge was, I couldn't work in television or film without getting into their Union.

As a hairstylist, I was meeting amazing people through my client referrals and connections. Those contacts snowballed into the jazz world. I became acquainted with notable musicians like bassists, "Ready" Freddie Washington, Nathan East and drum master, Leon Ndugu Chancler. I was introduced to Al Jarreau and Joe Sample and spent time with them while they were on tour. That was while I was vacationing in Japan, but that's another story.

Once settled in Los Angeles, while acquainting myself with the stars, I focused my time working my hairstyling magic on music videos, television commercials and advertising print work. I was on set during the Tony Terry video shoot, "When I'm with you." That video just happened to be Blair Underwood's directorial debut. As doors and arms opened to me, I began to work with entertainers like, Slick Rick, and hair styling album cover projects for Atlantic Star, Natalie Cole, Oleta Adams, and George Duke to name a few.

One afternoon, while I was styling George Duke's hair, Jeffrey Osborne dropped by the set. Jeffrey is also from Rhode Island, and he reminded me that our families knew one another. My favorite Aunt 'Laine (the professional singer) had known Jeffrey and his whole family since I was a small child. Before Jeffrey became a world celebrated vocalist, he was an incred ibly good drummer. I don't knowif people remember this, but Jeffrey Osborne was the drummer for the A&M group L.T.D before his big hit record of "Love Ballad." Later, he became a single artist with hit records like, "On the Wings of Love" and "I Really Don't Need No Light."

As I made in-roads into the Hollywood scene, I harbored a burning desire for more. I still needed to find a way to get necessary production hours. That affiliation would take me to the next level of my industry. My goal was to attain steady work in television and movies!

I tried networking. I would talk to film crew members in town, and I knocked on many doors. I was practically begging to get some insight on how to crack through the invisible walls restricting me. I needed a trusted break on how I could land a production job. I was laughed at by some. Some dismissed me like I was trash. Those hurtful feelings from my youth rose like Esophagitis. The pain burned in my chest. At those moments, I realized my feelings of being unacceptable, stemming from childhood, were still trapped inside. I squashed them, but they remained alive and well.

Working in Hollywood was a balancing act. You couldn't get in the Union without production hours. You couldn't get production hours without being in the union. There was no rule book or instructions on how to break the code. Never giving up, life was a constant working grind. Although the major gates remained locked, I was determined to find the keys. As always, I was fueled by my love for the work and a passion necessary to pursue my elusive dream.

CHAPTER SEVEN
"Game Changer"

There's something rooted in me about achieving the seemingly unimaginable. That resilience makes me realize that anything is possible. Just when I was about to give up, feeling as depleted as a month-old, helium birthday balloon, my 'woe-is-me moments' made a bright turn. On a regular day, without warning, a blessing came! In my typical conversation, with anyone who came across my path, I was always asking the same question. I was consistently working to get to the next level. I would ride by film crews and pull my car over, go by security, make my way to the hair trailer, and ask if they were hiring. In my effort to become a sought-after, Hollywood hairstylist, I was always hoping for some kind of breakthrough. This particular day, a makeup artist came out of a trailer to smoke a cigarette. Routinely, I walked over, realizing that subconsciously I was prepared to walk away, once again rejected. That's when I heard a voice say:

"*Hey kid, I've seen you hanging around these trailers on many occasions. I admire your persistence,*" he took a long drag from his cigarette and flicked the ashes on the ground.

"I'm going to give you a phone number that will give you all the information and requirements you need to become a union member. But don't tell anyone I gave you this number," he warned me.

"It's top-secret information," he said as he scribbled a phone number and a name on a scrap of paper, holding his cigarette securely between two fingers.

The name was Ilene Leonard, who at that time was in the contract legal services department of the 706 Union. The stranger handed me the paper gingerly, like it was a hundred-dollar bill he wasn't sure I deserved. Before he changed his mind, I grabbed it and thanked him profusely. I was thrilled for the opportunity and grateful for his goodwill. Since many years have passed by, with successful results, can tell you who that kind soul was. He was the makeup artist for Whoopi Goldberg. His name is Mike Germain.

After making that phone call, I now had solid union information and was eager to pursue and build on the requirements from that connection. Then, another blessing fluttered into my life, like a feather from the golden bird of abundance. Later that summer, I got wind that BET was transitioning from Washington, DC to Los Angeles. One of their projects was a variety talk show, Live From L.A. with Tanya Hart. BET was a Game Changer!! It was one of the most proud, professional moments of my career. That first big break is forever pierced in my memory-bank like a diamond stud. The competition was thick, but I was chosen from over 200 plus stylists.

My first interview was with an actress, director, and producer. I couldn't believe my eyes. I was sitting across from the gorgeous, Sheila Frazier, the actress who played the love interest in the movie Super Fly.

My second interview was with the talk show host, Tanya Hart. That interview was a hands-on, interactive approach. I had to wow her with a hairstyle. I knew this challenge was to see if I had the level of skill and technique to crush the job. I wasn't worried at all. I just got to work, doing what I do. Needless to say, I landed the job!

That fragment of time and conversation with Tanya Hart was comfortable, but so surreal. I felt how the enormity of this accomplishment was somehow about to change my life. Coupled with the professional exposure and the celebrity clientele, I knew this would parlay my career to limitless heights.

In the days to follow, God's Light was shining on me. The stars were aligned. Celebrities I had only dreamed about styling were now sitting in my chair. I had many unbelievable moments, conversations, and experiences. Guests included my childhood idols, Sammy Davis, Jr., and Diahann Carroll. I was amazed, that after crouching in front of our family television set, all those years ago, watching Diahann Carroll on the Julia Show, here she was in the flesh. I remember as a young boy, studying her appearance and clipping my aunt 'Laine's blond wig to mimic Diahann's hairdo. Now, I was personally styling Ms. Carroll's hair! It was blowing my mind. Others who got comfortable in my style chair were James Brown, Sidney Poitier, Cicely Tyson, The Pointer Sisters, Marilyn McCoo, and too many more to name.

As amazing as this BET opportunity was, I remained focused on the importance of the accumulation of production hours. Once my hours reached a certain number, I again tried to join the Union. I was shattered when I was told the hours accumulated weren't recognized by the Union. I couldn't get production hours working with this show. At that time, BET wasn't considered a recognized network. I didn't understand the difference between cable opposed to mainstream television. Without production hours, I was denied once again. I couldn't apply for a Union card. It was a frustrating process. How could I be so close, and yet so far from where I ultimately wanted to be? I thought to myself, is this God's sense of humor or is this going to be my recurring reality?

Speaking of 'game changers,' once back in Southern California, I was interested in having a relationship with my father. I had so many questions. Why wasn't he there for me in my young, tender years? Why did he and my mother dissolve their marriage. Why were our families so isolated and angry with each other?

In 1985, ten years after I last saw my dad, things had changed drastically. Now, my father had remarried. He had changed religions and joined his new wife in becoming a Jehovah Witness. Luke Tunstall had turned his life around. Everything my brother had been telling me about my father, all the pictures I had painted in my mind, were not at all what I experienced or what I expected. The first thing that surprised me was that he had a three-year-old child by the name of Octavia. I had a little sister. In 1975, I had been looking for a friend in my father. He had other ideas. He was looking to be a father to me, a disciplinarian, and we clashed. Now, a decade later, we could sit down and talk, man-to-man.

I learned that my father was not a bum, like my mother and her relatives had tried to infer. He was a wonderful, hardworking, very loving man. He finally told me why he hadn't seen me in fifteen years. My father said he caught my mother having an affair with a man he thought was his best friend. It was the same guy I remembered, who made me, and my brother attend that Catholic School so many years ago. My father said he wanted to kill them both for their supreme betrayal. My dad's mother, realizing her son was wild with rage and capable of murder, sent him to live in California, as an effort to keep him out of jail. No wonder the families were not close. That was a terrible secret for them to have kept all these years.

My father said, over time, he did attempt to see me and my brother. He reached out to my mother, but she would never let that happen. E.P.T. never told us any part of that story. But, hearing my father's explanation for his strange disappearance from our lives helped heal a deep wound in my soul. Slowly, we began to rebuild our relationship. Love heals all.

Discovering his side of what happened and why his marriage dissolved, was an eye-opener. After my father explained his absence from my life, it forced me to gaze into my own mirror. I had fathered two young children back in Rhode Island, three-thousand-miles from where I lived. I didn't want to make the same mistakes my father had.

Diligently, I made every attempt not to repeat the same behavior that I had once condemned. I stepped up to my responsibility as a father to my daughter, my first-born child. But I was young, and I wasn't ready for marriage. When we broke up, my teenage sweetheart met someone who wanted to marry her. Once they tied the knot, although I struggled to be in my child's life, for a time, I lost contact with them. My little girl was almost twelve when we finally reunited.

In 1985, when I decided to relocate to California, I invited the mother of my first-born son to join me. Her mother had relocated to Florida, and she was getting up-there in age.

Consequently, that mother of my child chose to move to Florida and care for her parent. No worries. I was hopping on planes, going back and forth to Florida, to stay in my son's life. I've focused on maintaining a relationship with my children, because of what happened between me and my father. I vowed to God and myself, never to repeat that mistake.

CHAPTER EIGHT
"Full Circle"

A well known Candidate for the Senator's race was attending a fundraiser. At the last minute, her hairstylist took ill. One of the crew members, who happened to be a friend of mine, overheard the conversation, and recommended her assistant call me. Without hesitation, I was available to meet the demand. Like Clark Kent, with an ever-ready cape on my back, I was called upon to save the day. I knew the experience was an opportunity for me to expand my vision to include soliciting an even higher-end clientele. That's exactly how things worked out.

At the time, I worked at Cliques in Beverly Hills, until that Salon abruptly shut down. Just like that, I was without employment and in need of another steady cash flow. One thing I did have as collateral, was my extensive clientele. I don't know if it was a courageous move or an unintelligent one, but again, I took a leap of faith. I moved from a one-bedroom apartment to an extraordinarily luxurious penthouse suite in the heart of the mid-Wilshire-district of Los Angeles. The building was complete with high-end amenities (valet, security, fitness) and the ambiance was off-the-chart. My place had a view like no other! Literally, I could see the culturally iconic and historic Hollywood sign from my balcony.

My rent went from 650-dollars to over 1,200-dollars a month. At the time, I didn't know where the funds would come from to afford such a place. I stood on my beautiful patio, staring out at the Hollywood sign, and holding onto one of my favorite mantras; *"All things are possible to those who believe."*

California taught me that dual careers were essential to survive. It took skill, talent, and fortitude to balance the high cost of living on the sunny West Coast with my fluctuating income. Fortunately, I had experience as a barber, a hairstylist, and an educator. I didn't mind working long hours. When you love what you do, it doesn't feel like work. My days were fueled by my passion and love for my craft.

Thankfully, job offers were in abundance for both television and print ads. I moved and expanded my business from a private hair studio to a six-chair salon. My vision of success continued coming to fruition.

As faith would have it, the assistant from the Senator's fundraiser had become one of my recurring clients. When she came to get her hair done at my new penthouse salon, she was impressed with the layout. I watched her as she slowly surveyed the many celebrity photos on my wall. It was obvious she was intrigued by my lifestyle and by me.

"What do you want to accomplish with your career?" she inquired.

I discussed my frustration with production hours and trying to get into the Hollywood Union for hair stylists.

"Do you know what I do for a living?" She quickly responded as I styled her hair.

"Yes, you manage the Senator's fundraising events," I answered, carefully sweeping my comb through her locks.

Unbeknownst to me, my client was the Director of the Hair, Make up and Wardrobe Department at ABC studios. My classy client asked me for my resumé and I happily obliged. She was kind enough to slip my resumé into her purse. However, she explained there was a hiring freeze at her network. Still, she assured me that when the freeze was lifted, I should be looking for a call. True to her words, the call did come. I was informed I had an upcoming interview with an ABC supervisor. As a result of that meeting, the supervisor was impressed with my level of experience, my accomplishments, style, and confidence. That supervisor was eager to let me know she would have aposition coming up in a few months.

"However," she mused. "I would like to hire you in the interim for a special project. You're in my top three picks," her secret smile teased me.

Well, the "top-secret" project happened to be The Academy Awards hair team! As if that wasn't enough of an amazing blessing, she casually mentioned that one of her employees was going on maternity leave.

"Can you get up at 5am?" she queried.

"Can I ever!" I assured my new boss that if she, in fact, hired me, I would not let her down.

"Yes, I will get up and I will show up!" I replied. "I'll be on time and before time."

The next thing I knew, I had landed the job as part of the popular television show, General Hospital! This sky-rocketed my level in the industry. I was making 150-dollars per day with BET. At ABC I was making twenty-nine dollars an hour, with benefits. Importantly, I was now able to gain true production hours and to finally join the elusive Union.

The first day I worked on the set of General Hospital, during my 30-minute lunch break, I sat quietly on the sound stage, meditating in the dark. I just wanted to be in the moment and consider my many blessings. After a while, I pulled out my cell phone and called my mother. My emotions spilled over, and I could barely get my voice to speak. I was so emotional that day, I started crying when I heard my mother's caring voice.

E.P.T said, *"What's the matter son?"*

could hear the concern in her voice, and I wanted to reassure her that my tears were joyful.

"Mom, what did I tell you as a child that I would do one day? Do you remember when I said I would be working with celebrities?" I didn't give her time to answer.

"What's your favorite soap opera?" I demanded.

She replied, *"Stop playing games, boy. You know it's General Hospital."*

"You will never guess where I'm standing right now! I'm on the sound stage of General Hospital. Mom, my dreams are becoming a reality. I want you to come to California and see for yourself. I brought you a plane ticket to come out next week," I told her with excitement in my voice.

She was in shock, but I had more surprises for her. While I was talking to my mother, one of the main stars had walked up to me on the dark sound stage.

I said, *"Hold on, Ma,"* and I handed Stuart Damon, (a/k/a Alan Quartermaine) the phone. He graciously spoke a few pleasantries to my mother. She was over the moon with excitement. When he handed back my cell phone, E.P.T. blurted out, *"Son, I always knew you would be something. But I didn't know you would be on the set of General Hospital. I had no idea you would succeed like this. You've made me a believer that dreams do come true. Continue dreaming, son."*

I told her I would see her next week and to start packing. Then I hung up. My break was over, and it was time to get back to work.

One thing I've learned about life, for every gain there's a challenge to overcome. Time on the set of General Hospital wasn't completely welcoming. As a black stylist, I was prematurely judged by the crew. Some doubted my ability to be knowledgeable about all kinds of hair and hair styles. Once again, I was having to prove myself. That brought me to another flashback, feeling rejected by Arthur Angelo's Academy. In my prestigious job, I still had to prove myself, work harder, keep me temperament in check and maintain a pleasant demeanor. In Hollywood, you don't ever want to appear to be that angry black man. I did my job well and carried on with a prayer in my heart that *"this too shall pass."*

One of the leading actresses, Jane Elliot, had a thick, healthy, but coarse head of hair that took forever to blow dry. One unexpected day, her hairdresser was out sick. Confident and opportunistic, I quickly offered to step in and take on the challenge. I assured my supervisor I could cut, and blow dry her hair in half the time they were used to. Initially, Ms. Elliot was reluctant to allow someone that she wasn't familiar with to style her hair. Nevertheless, somewhat sarcastically she said, *"So I'm told you can cut, and blow dry my hair in half the time?"* she posed it as a question, but I knew it had now become a challenge.

I smiled my winning smile and got to work. I did cut her blow dry time in half. Magically, a transformation happened before everyone's eyes. Her mane of hair was smooth, silky, and polished. She was way more impressed than I had expected. The result was pleasing to my professional ego.

The other lead actresses came bouncing into the hair room, along with the background actress I had styled earlier that day. They were all asking the same question.

"Who did her hair?"

I knew my success wouldn't go over well with everyone, because some of the other hair stylists were temperamental and insecure. I thought they might have found themselves slightly intimidated and perhaps even jealous. Then, someone threw me under the bus and blurted out, *"Brian did her hair."*

A little later, I was summoned to meet with my supervisor. I must admit I was paranoid thinking, oh, I'm in trouble now. Talk about the 'long' walk of uncertainty towards her closed door. My heart was pounding against my chest and my palms were sweating as I approached my supervisor's office. I was trying to recollect every encounter I had experienced with the crew and any strained situations that had come up over the past couple of days. I was in defense mode when I arrived at her door and pushed it open.

Unbeknownst to me, the starlet, Emma Sams, had called my supervisor and requested I do her hair. Straight away, my supervisor babbled a succession of compliments that took me completely off-guard. It took me a minute to grasp what she was saying. Emma Sams wanted me to work on her hair. She said the secondary actress, whose hair I styled earlier, notably stood out from the lead actress. Emma Sams said she wanted me to style her hair and she wanted her mane to radiate in the same beautiful way.

I learned a valuable lesson that day. You never style the background actor's hair better than the lead actor. Another thing I noted was that the crew was starting to pay close attention to Brian Andrew and his impeccable work.

CHAPTER NINE
"Surreal Joy"

The 62nd Academy Awards, held in 1990, was hosted by Billy Crystal. That night, Denzel Washington won the Oscar for Best Supporting Actor in "Glory" and "Driving Miss Daisy" won Best Picture.

The weeks leading up to that Academy Awards show, I was filled with an excitement like no other. I was honored to have been selected for such a prestigious platform to showcase my talent.

Fashion designer Keiko Mareno, from Rhode Island, dressed me for the event. She presented several custom-made pieces, and I chose the outfit that screamed "proud moment." She custom tailored it justfor me.

The evening was Magical! I continuously reminded myself to, 'pause, breathe and focus.' That was my "keep-composure-mindset," to restrain myself from being so incredibly star-struck.

Going through security and the badge process was intimidating. A frightening wave of insecurity swirled around me when I arrived. It was as if I was in an interrogation room or a criminal line-up. However, the second I received that privileged badge, a wave of emotion rattled me. I felt so grateful, as I flashed back to the years of grind and preparation that got me to this very moment.

On a break, I called my brother, Junie, and my Aunt Elaine. I had to share my excitement with my family. My voice squealed with elation, while giving them the blow-by-blow, impending chain of events to come.

Back on my job, in rapid succession, I was seeing one celebrity after another. It was a behind-the-scenes, ordered chaos that fueled a fast and furious production. Keeping up with the pace and responding to my client needs, I gave them my best, in a confident, professional way. The pressure was piercing, but I focused and embraced the madness. People from Jamie Lee Curtis to Quincy Jones and Harrison Ford were standing directly in front of me. If that star-power wasn't enough to pull my attention away from my work, there were beautiful women floating past my chair and smiling my way. Many were super stars like the late Ruby Dee and the dynamic Cicely Tyson, to name a few. I recall sharing an elevator with Richard Gere, who complimented me on my suit saying I looked Dapper! I couldn't believe that the lead actor in 'American Gigolo' was giving me a compliment. When I raced into the men's room, I saw Alan Thicke walk into the stall next to mine. Everywhere I turned, I was surrounded by super-stars.

Once I calmed down, I easily settled into my position as a B team hairstylist. I had been hired to style hair downstairs, servicing the dancers and presenters. Russel Smith, who ran the hair team, quickly noticed how professionally I carried myself. When he saw my custom-tailored outfit and noticed the way I performed under pressure, he elevated me to the A team. These were hair stylists stationed stage-side and doing last minute touch-ups for host, Billy Crystal and all the other presenters. Our precise make-up and hair adjustments happened before they went on stage.

After my performance at this 62nd Academy Award event, I had the honor of being asked to return. I happily participated as part of the Academy Award team for the next four years. This was extremely prestigious, because at that time, I was the only black male to have worked on the Academy Awards Hair Team. At some of the future Oscar award shows, I had the pleasure of meeting the phenomenal Debbie Allen, who choreographed the Awards that year. I attended the Oscar After-Party she hosted. I didn't stay long; just enough time to star-gaze the room, have a glass of champagne and end my evening on a cloud.

After meeting Debbie Allen, we continued collaborating. I had the pleasure of being part of her hair team in 2002, while working with Ms. Allen on her Daytime Emmy nominated show, "Cool Women." The employment offers kept rolling in. I've worked on just about every prestigious award show in Hollywood. That includes the Emmy Awards, The NAACP Image Awards, the American Music Awards and I worked on the Golden Globes. As the accolades grew and my career blossomed, I turned once again to my faith. *"If ye have faith as a grain of mustard seed, ye shall say unto this mountain, remove hence to yonder place; and it shall remove, and nothing shall be impossible. Matthew 17:20*

CHAPTER TEN

"Credentials in Hand"

A long-awaited achievement was finally accomplished. I accumulated the required hours to join the Union. I had some minor loose ends to tighten- up, including completion of the paperwork, but that didn't take long. Finally, I was officially a member of the I.A.T.S.E (International Alliance of Theatrical Stage Employees), Local 706. Mission accomplished, right?

Well, I didn't realize the Union dues were so expensive. In a panic, I managed to scrounge up the lump sum of money needed and paid my dues immediately to avoid any further barrier in meeting my goal.

Oh, what a feeling! My first Union meeting. I was sworn in. I was somewhat nervous over the anticipation of the process and excited by the opportunity to meet my peers. It was thrilling to belong to a Union of respected colleagues in the industry. As I was being sworn in, I surveyed the room. Surprisingly, the lack of black or brown people present made a haunting and blatant unspoken statement.

I quickly realized that the Union had varying levels of superiority. The Journeyman credentials were the pinnacle for a Hairstylist. I left that meeting, keen to research how I could achieve my next level. Although, there was no time frame to accomplish it, I set my sights on my next project; that of becoming a Journeyman. It was a "no brainer" for me. Without this prestigious credential, work opportunities and my bank account would not be as lucrative. No Journeyman status would equal less income. I wanted no holdbacks. No obstacles! If there was an opportunity to reach a higher level, I was wholeheartedly up for the challenge. With a "must-win, will-win" attitude, I remained focused and studied for the entry exam.

It was an intense curriculum. I took many classes before I could schedule an exam date. This preparation for the Journeyman exam was serious business.

Classes were costly. I purchased the "bible" book for hairstylists; The Corsen Book. Additionally, I knew I needed direction and maybe even tutoring. I started looking around for the perfect person to help me.

Angels have a way of appearing in my life every time I start to reach a point of weariness and distraction. One angel was Deborah Dobson, a Department Head for Hair during my time at General Hospital. She was instrumental in providing valuable information and direction that assisted me with my study techniques. She also helped me put together my Time Period Kit. This kit is needed for the hands-on, live presentation that occurs during the exam process.

One of the instructors of an exam prep class was the late, Peggy Shannon. Ms. Shannon was one of the Union's first elite, stellar and well- respected Hair supervisors. She worked in television and film for decades. Her celebrity included working with the likes of historic actresses like Bette Davis. Lucky for me, Peggy took an immediate liking to me. She admired the passion I exhibited for my craft and graciously took me under her wing. It was her tutelage that helped provide me with a certain understanding of the pins, hair pieces, and wigs from the late 1500's to the present. She masterfully understood and interpreted the bi-laws, rules, and regulations that Journeymen needed to know. I discovered that Robert Louis Stevenson was one of the first African American hair stylists in the Union. Ms. Shannon shared this information with me and suggested that proud piece of black history was a reference point for me. She thought I displayed a similarity to Mr. Stevenson, who had broken color-barriers in the Hollywood Union.

That piqued my interest, so I did a little research and discovered that Robert Louis Stevenson was hired as the first African American, male hair stylist in Hollywood around 1969. After him, an African American woman named Bernadine Anderson, a make-up expert, broke the color barrier when she became Jane Fonda's personal assistant for eight years. She also did make-up for Eddie Murphy and all his doubles.

In the late sixties, long before I arrived on the Hollywood scene, the Equal Employment Opportunity Commission published a study that highlighted discrimination in the film business. There were over 19,000 folks employed in Hollywood, working behind the scenes. Only 400 of those people were minorities and their jobs were lower level, like clerical and janitorial. Mr. Robert Louis Stevenson said it took him two years to work his way into the 706 Union, even though he was an accomplished hairstylist. He recognized that I. A. T. S. E. Union especially needed his talents, the same way they needed me. Why? Because African American actors and actresses wanted make-up specialists and hair stylists who understood how to apply their make-up and people who were familiar and trained in styling black hair. Like Robert Louis Stevenson, I studied to be a master of both. Also, like Mr. Stevenson, we were both equipped with the knowledge and practice of styling white hair. Unlike many of our peers, who could only style Caucasian hair, we mastered all ethnic hair styles. You don't know how many horror stories I've heard from prominent African American actresses about their terrible encounters with hair stylists who burned their scalps or could not manage their hair properly.

Being an understudy of Peggy Shannon was a privilege. She was my trusted mentor. Peggy believed in my instincts, my skills and encouraged my creativity. I practiced repeatedly on my ethnic model because I knew that's where I was needed. Until one unexpected afternoon, I was approached by another Journeyman. That person offered me seemingly helpful advice. He discouraged me from using an ethnic model and told me I should use a Caucasian model, otherwise my talents would be frowned upon.

My impulse was to take note of this advice. After all, my skills had always been challenged when it came to my ability to style various ethnic hair. The first thing they want to ask you is, can you style the white actresses? Of course, I can! I was well versed and excellent working with all kinds of hair and skin tones. Still, because of this person's comments I altered my vision and began working with a white model. When my new model appeared, Ms. dumbfounded. She wanted to know why I had changed my vision. I told her about the "tip" I had received and the warning that I was setting myself up for failure. Needless to say, this infuriated her.

"How dare that person have the audacity to make that comment to you," she was seething.

My kind-hearted mentor was so bothered by this turn of events; she contacted the union president. Peggy thought the advice I had received was discriminatory and racist. She felt a complaint should be made. The President of the Union acted quickly and called me personally to inquire about the incident. We had a long conversation. However, I stepped away from that phone call feeling disappointed. It was unsettling. Instead of the support and concern I expected, I was encouraged to understand the politics of the Union. He suggested I know my place and position, then navigate accordingly. It was made perfectly clear, the union preferred not dealing with rumbles of complaints and unfairness. He advised I pick and choose my battles wisely. Suddenly, I felt I was in a Catch-22 situation. I'd be damned if I did and damned if I didn't. It was another wake-up call for me. I thought about what Mr. Stevenson had gone through to become a journeyman in the Hollywood union. It appeared some things had not changed, even though it was half a century later.

After things settled down, Ms. Shannon was adamant when she told me, *"It doesn't matter what color you are. Your talent will shine in a color-blind way. Stay true to yourself."*

Her counsel and support were invaluable, but I also recognized that Peggy Shannon probably had no idea what people of color were up against when it came to ascending the ladder of success. We live inside an America where bigotry and systemic racism still flourish. It wasn't the Journeymen's card that would change things for me. It was the mindset of many in white America that had to change.

Unselfishly, my mentor continued to teach me important finishing tricks and tools. Peggy shared part of her arsenal of hair secrets. We trained diligently together, even on the weekends. She pushed me hard and Iembraced every lesson from a place of gratitude.

Exam day quickly approached. I displayed a confident, exterior demeanor, but inside my stomach was tied in knots. I did believe my hard work and preparation would pay off. I never doubted that. I believed in myself and my skills. However, I was still nervous. I knew the mountain I had to climb was in that room and beyond. What I had to overcome was racism.

The mood in the testing room was tenuous and anxious. People were physically nervous, with hands notably trembling. Some even packed up their belongings, before the exam had even started, and left the room. I suppose they were feeling unprepared and second -guessing themselves.

The exam lasted two-days, 10-hours a day, featuring a live, hands-on presentation. We were graded on our set up, how expeditiously we performed and how precise we were. We were judged on wig techniques and hair styling for various time periods in American history. The period pieces were only acknowledged on that specific examination day, and we were graded accordingly. My weeks of study paid off. I passed the exam.

Once I became a full-fledged Journeyman, I was still naive in understanding the industry. My prestigious credential gave me false expectations. For example, I thought I would be offered the stellar levels of work within the industry. I was mistaken. Those were slow in coming. My success, instead, was a double-edged sword. I soon discovered some of my peers were intimidated by my accomplishments. Many of my colleagues had been in the industry for years. Quite a few were too brow-beaten and afraid to take the Journeyman exam. Consequently, they settled into the comfortable, lower levels of their craft. Others had failed the test two or three times. I, on the other hand, came back to my job feeling proud that I had conquered yet another personal goal on the very first try. Plus, I was one of the youngest black, male Journeymen at that time. Believe me, I felt the icy cold reserve emanating from my mostly white peers.

Still, I stood proud. I was elevating in a multi-level playing field, because of my many faceted skill sets. Not only had I become a Journeyman, but I was also a master barber, an in-demand hairstylist, highly skilled in all hair types, lengths, and textures, as well as competent in styling wigs, hair pieces, extensions and well versed in Special Effects hair styling. Special Effects wasn't even acategory until I arrived on the scene.

In other words, I had reached a certain plateau in my craft. It was difficult for some of my peers to accept that a black man had made such headway. To my disappointment, I became a threat instead of a co-worker.

I've never been a selfish person and I enjoy being a team player. I desired to see my co-workers gain their own notoriety. I've always had a benevolent mindset, so it was inevitable that I'd begin helping others reach their full potential. I think of myself as a natural born teacher. The same way Peggy had encouraged and taught me; I began to share with others. I provided study guides and free training classes to several top hair stylists. Typically, this type of training, like what Peggy Shannon shared with me, would cost $200 dollars an hour. But I wanted to give back. My lessons were meant to be of service to others. I targeted those who have been in the industry for over 25 years and those who were still at an entry level, stylist position. I walked the walk and ignored the talk.

One thing being a Journeyman did change. My phone was buzzing with new business. I was offered key, new products to utilize, and I found myself working on the sets of major movies. As I slid into major network studios, it was only a matter of time before I encountered new challenges. With each achievement came new obstacles. Politics were politics and systemic racism was vividly alive. My blackness seemed to be a threat.

My name and impressive credentials were published (without a photograph) and added to every new assignment list provided by the Union. Many days, I would arrive at my early morning work call for a major show. I believe, some people didn't know me and had only heard my name. With so many credentials, most assumed I was Caucasian. So, when I would show-up at 5:30am, ahead of time and prepared to work, suddenly, I'd be told, *"We overbooked the job and will not need your services."*

I think back to a specific, hurtful time when one morning I knocked on the appropriate trailer door and announced myself. The woman who opened the door looked me up and down, then assumed I was working in another capacity and said, *"You need to sign in around the corner."*

"I'm here as the hairstylist," I politely let her know she was mistaken.

Well, her expression was frozen in place. She told me to wait outside. The trailer door was shut in my face and when she returned, at least five minutes later, the stranger had my start-up paperwork in hand.

"You can fill out this paperwork and go home," she told me. *"We'll pay you for the day. We overbooked."*

At first, that became the norm for most of the union calls I received. As sickening and equally disappointing as that was, my persistence was unwavering. This stubborn man was determined they would not strip me of my dignity or my obligation to feed myself and my family. After all, I was serious about taking care of the children I had fathered, and I was diligent about paying child support. I was also just as serious about doing my job and doing it well.

As luck would have it, I received a call from three important union hair stylists: Julia Walker, Joanne Stafford-Chaney, and Robert Louis Stevenson. Each one offered me work on my first major, feature film as a hairstylist. The cast was huge. It was "Sister Act 2, Back in the Habit" starring Whoopi Goldberg, Maggie Smith, Barnard Hughes, Kathy Najimy, and Mary Wickes. Julia wanted to add me to her team. I was offered the same opportunity to team up with Joanne Stafford-Chaney and likewise for Robert Louis Stevenson, the very man Peggy Shannon had compared me to when I was striving to become a Local 706 Union member. Recently, Mr. Stevenson received a Lifetime Achievement Award from our union in 2018.

Believe me, I was trying to strategize and find a way to work with all three of these legendary individuals. The reality was, I couldn't be in three places at once. I had to pick a lane. The opportunities presented by all three were great. After much deliberation, I chose to walk with Joanne. I knew that she was busy and my affiliation with her could open new doors of opportunity. I was right. After my big break on that major film, I was called to work on several television sitcoms. They included, *Thea,* starring Thea Vidale, Brandy Norwood, Jason Weaver, Brenden Jefferson, and Yvette Wilson. Next came the extremely popular television series, *Living Single*, that featured Queen Latifah, Kim Coles, Erika Alexander, Terrence C. Carson, Kim fields, Mel Jackson, and John Henton. The third show was *Hanging with Mr. Cooper.* Once again, I was surrounded by a star-studded cast including Raven- Symone, Mark Curry, Omar Gooding, and Holly Robinson Peete.

The sitcoms were the golden ticket. Joanne Stafford-Chaney was instrumental in my true entryway to solid union work. She was the original Department Head Hairstylist for all three projects. I felt like I had won the lottery.

One of my signature beliefs is always to be ready! When Joanne had to temporarily relocate, due to family issues, she went to the producers on my behalf. Because of my work ethics and because Joanne requested that I hold her position down as the Department Head for Hairstyling, I got the gig for all three shows. It was unheard of for someone so young in the union to be a Department Head. Nevertheless, I accepted the position and became very busy overseeing those three hair departments. Boy, did that create a shake-up in our union politics.

In between sitcom-seasons, I was getting calls for film work. I landed a couple of major movie opportunities and worked on the sitcom, *Sister, Sister,* featuring the twins, Tia and Tamera Mowry, Tim Reid, Jackée Harry, and Marques Houston. All these amazing things were starting to happen in my career. Clearly, my due diligence and dedication to my craft was finally paying off. I was living thejourney of my dreams!

One morning while on the set of *Sister, Sister*, I received a phone call from a legend in our make-up and hair style business, Ronald Smith. He styled such people as Duke Ellington, Cab Calloway, Lena Horne, and many others. Ron was excited to share a big opportunity with me; one that he assured would deliver a stairway to the stars. He thought it could be a pinnacle opportunity to elevate my career.

I hesitated because the sitcoms were a blessing. They provided stability, a great work environment, an appreciation for my leadership and a comfortable, working crew. The new opportunity was to move from my sitcoms to episodic work on *Star Trek: Deep Space Nine*. The lead actor was Mr. Avery Brooks. Also, I would be working under the amazing tutelage of Department Head, Josie Norman, and renowned hairstylist, Norma Lee. They were staples in our industry and highly respected. This offer included a multi-seasonal contract, a multi-cultural work environment and the pay was awesome. I would become part of the crew on one of the biggest, most recognized television shows of all time. *The Star Trek* world was hugely popular! I spent a few sleepless nights, weighing my options. In the end, I made the move.

I was beyond excited to be working on such a prestigious show. I have been an enthusiast of Mr. Brooks since his days as Hawk in the 1985 – 1988 television series, *Spenser for Hire* and his own hit spin-off television show, *A Man called Hawk*. It was my great honor to become the personal hairstylist to Mr. Avery Brooks, who played the part of Captain Benjamin Sisko on *Star Trek: Deep Space Nine*. Mr. Brooks is a wise and influential man. I appreciated his professional interest in me. He was always pushing me towards excellence. As an educator and successful industry example, he taught me that words matter, but your actions matter more. I would hang onto each of his wisdom-words and received his advice with gratitude.

In 2000, I interviewed for a hairstylist position for one of the most highly anticipated remakes of a movie, "*How the Grinch Stole Christmas*." Over two hundred hairstylists interviewed, and I was the 7th selected out of the forty finally chosen. To say I was up for the challenge is an understatement. This was a dream-come-true job that gave me the freedom to be as creative as I wished to be. It was thrilling and challenging to design wigs in a very imaginative way that portrayed each unusual character. I explored my unique abilities with an open, child's heart. You could have likened me to a kid playing with crayons and an Aladdin coloring book. I was imagining my own magic carpet ride. My experience on the set of "How the Grinch Stole Christmas" was nothing short of supernatural. Every ounce of study from my days preparing for the journeyman exam was captured and applied during my work. That film was a fulfilling professional experience. We all felt so validated when the hair and make-up team won an Oscar that year.

Admiringly, this allowed me the opportunity to work with Ron Howard. I grew up watching him on television as part of the "Happy Days" cast and on the popular "Andy Griffith Show." Now, he was an award-winning producer director "The Grinch who Stole Christmas became another plume in his industry cap. Director Ron Howard appeared as a 'Whoville police character' in a crowd scene of the movie.

Once again, I was the only black male hairstylist on the set. I was joined by only one other black woman make-up expert out of a whole make-up department. As awesome as this experience was, I had my own personal concerns. I quietly swallowed the bitter pill that racism and discrimination was still present within the hiring practices of Hollywood.

Because I carried myself with confidence, some of my peers assumed I was arrogant. Not true. Yet, clearly, I intimidated a few of my colleagues, simply because I was young, gifted, and black. The heaviness of that burden, on what should have been one of my more special and memorable experiences haunts me to this day.

Around this same time, my love interest went into premature labor. I was working on this film called "Love & Basketball" when she drove up to the studio to swoop me up. We rushed to the hospital. My son was born prematurely. He coded, but the doctors brought him back.

He had to stay in the (NICU) Neonatal Intensive Care Unit, until he was strong enough to come home. One thing I have learned from that stressful and emotional situation. All our lives are full of challenges and obstacles. You can never really tell what people are going through by looking at them. At my job, I appeared normal, professional and in control. But inside, I was anxious and worried for the two weeks that tiny, little boy was fighting for his life in the hospital. His mother and I could finally exhale, once we cuddled him into his blue, cotton blanket and brought him home.

It's true, with the escalating good times came some disappointing moments. But again, I am the grandson of the late, Pop, Red Smith, and the son of Luke Tunstall II. If they could stay focused and achieve success, against all odds, so could I! Many a day, I relied on the endless scriptures rooted in my soul. They have always carried me forward in knowing:

"Yea ... I will fear no evil, for thou art with me. Thy rod and thy staff they comfort me. Thou preparest a table before me in the presence of my enemies. Thou anointest my head with oil. My cup runneth over."

Psalm 23:4-5

CHAPTER ELEVEN
"Epiphany"

I'm sure we all remember where we were when we heard the news Michael Jackson had died. The world mourned his death and was shocked into silence at his passing. He was one of the most significant cultural figures of the 20th century and one of the greatest entertainers in the history of music.

At home, eyes glued to my television set, I watched the news in disbelief. I recall casually talking with my youngest son and saying how incredible it would be if we were invited to the M. J. Memorial. The very second after saying this, my phone rang. On the other line was the makeup artist for the Jackson family. I gave her my condolences and we discussed the loss of an icon. To my surprise, she invited me to participate in his historically important memorial. That's how I became part of the hair and makeup team. Out of all the hairstylists in the union, to be chosen for Michael's exclusive celebration of life was an extraordinary and humbling moment. To become part of this historic occasion was mind-blowing. I knew I would be connecting with some of the finest young music moguls, as well as seasoned icons of the entertainment industry. It was a dream-like experience.

Although I never worked directly on styling Michael, I was in his company on several occasions. We crossed paths at the Grammy's, the American Music Awards, at Motown 25 and Motown 30 reunions.

Now, I would be a part of his lifetime celebration and worldwide tribute.

The Michael Jackson memorial was like nothing I had ever experienced. It's emblazoned in my memory. It was July 7, 2009, in Los Angeles, California. You had to have confidential credentials to bypass the top-secret security at the Staple Center. In front of the venue sat an endless procession of state trooper vehicles, noticeably present. I heard that over 3,000 officers were on duty that day. I had to arrive way earlier than the 10:30AM scheduled start-time for the memorial event. As usual, I was early, completely set-up and ready to work.

Around ten-o-clock, Michael Jackson's closed, bronze casket arrived. It was rumored that the casket was 14K gold-plated. The $25,000 final resting place for Michael was decorated with a huge burst of red roses and Bells of Ireland flowers. They settled it down, directly in front of the stage, that was also over-flowing with flower arrangements. All of Michael's brothers arrived, wearing a single, white, sequined glove to tribute Michael. They were seated in the front row.

I had my wave of nerves throughout the day but managed to keep my emotions in check. So many in attendance were still stunned by the loss of Michael Jackson and overcome with sorrow. I too felt a deep sense of grief.

During that sad occasion, I saw a parade of important people like actress, rapper, singer, Queen Latifah and Michael's back-up singer, who sang duets with him in preparation for his final tour, Judith Hill. Seasoned R&B icons were present like Lionel Richie, his daughter Nicole, (who, I was told, was Michael's Goddaughter), Smokey Robinson, Usher, Jennifer Hudson, Akon, and pop icon Mariah Carey, who sang "I'll Be There," as a duet with Trez Lorenz.

The Andrae Crouch choir performed, and Christian ministers blessed the event with their presence. Pastor Lucious Smith prayed, and Martin Luther King III was there, as was Rev. Jessie Jackson and Rev. Al Sharpton. Actress, Brooke Shields was present and a host of sport stars like Kobe Bryant and Magic Johnson.

I saw rapper/producer Sean P. Diddy Combs walking around. The Commodores group attended and so many more. But I was particularly overwhelmed with respect, when I saw Motown royalty in the house like record company founder, Berry Gordy, Smokey Robinson, Suzanne de Passe, and the great Stevie Wonder. However, I was somewhat surprised by something that transpired backstage.

Here I was, a hairstylist, doing my job and working with these luminaries and legends in an expansive work area. Into my workspace walks Smokey Robinson, inquiring about his green room and a place where he could change his clothes. Well, they hadn't provided a dressing room for Mr. Robinson or Mr. Gordy. Shockingly, neither of them had their own designated rooms in that entire, expansive Staple Center. I thought it was ridiculous that no rooms had been provided for them and I voiced my opinion about that quite loudly. It touched a nerve in me. These promoters knew Michael's musical history and his roots. So how could they not recognize the value of those who mentored Michael Jackson?

The organizers of the event made excuses and said they had run out of rooms. So, after much back and forth with the people who were controlling the event-planning, I offered to share my space with the Motown legends. I had the engineers put up some partitions to create rooms. That way, Smokey Robinson, Mr. Gordy, and Suzanne de Passe could have an area where they could entertain guests, change clothes, and have some privacy to meet and greet. It just seemed like the right thing to do.

The legends thanked me, but I was happy to do it. One thing, I know for sure. We must never forget our history and the importance and respect that goes together with every legacy. After all, if it were not for Suzanne de Passe and Mr. Gordy discovering the Jackson 5, there would be no Michael Jackson. Thankfully, it all worked out fine.

At the end of my day, when I walked back to my car, happily drained, I was very emotional because of the immeasurable love and fellowship I had witnessed in that auditorium.

All who participated in that memorial will forever share a special bond. The music, the memoires of the man and the love that surrounded him will eternally touch our hearts and the hearts of the world.

CHAPTER TWELVE
"Just Can't Catch a Break"

Just when I thought my career couldn't get any better the next blessing was a working position on the television show, "ER!" This time, I was delegated as the Department Head. Dare I say COLOSSAL?! One of Warner Brother's Greatest hit series accelerated me to a new status position. It was an enormously proud moment.

Then came an emergency phone call from home. Calamity hits again! My mother called from Rhode Island to sadly inform me my stepfather had died from Cancer. I immediately flew home to Providence. The tall order before me was to help my mother balance her emotional grief and the burial business, while under a serious constraint of time. After all, I would have to be away from the set of "ER" and I was the Department Head. Every second was thought out and well-planned to accomplish what needed to be done. At that moment, family first was my motto.

Once arriving in Providence, I recognized for the first time, that my mother's home was antiquated and needed to be renovated. Nothing was working properly. Not only was it a blinding eye-sore on the block, it was not supportive of her failing health challenges. I discovered my mother's mobility was fragile. She needed a handicapped accessible home. I immediately attacked the problem. First, I secured her at a nearby hotel until the renovations were completed.

Honestly, I had no idea where to start, or what to do. But being the self-made man that I am, the work proceeded. Without a negative thought, I started knocking down walls. Who knew I had carpenter skills? My beloved, jack-of-all-trades grandfather must have been resting on my shoulders, whispering in my ear, and providing me the direction and patience I needed. Certainly, I had never done such renovation. I tackled sheet rock and ceilings. I was hammering and hiking up and down ladders. My whole body ached from dragging material in and out of the house with due diligence. After a time, I recruited a couple of friends to help with small projects. That quickly expanded into a full hands-on renovation. We made Home Depot store runs several times a day. Trial and error insisted I master matric moments, measurements, painting, and a whole lot of do- overs. I pushed my body to a fatigue that was both exhilarating and exhausting.

Thankfully, my mother loved the renovations. I'm not sure if I heard all the great things she had to say about my work, because I was so proud of what I accomplished, I kept talking over her compliments. Maybe I was full of myself and a bit braggadocious! But that experience was another reminder of how good God is and that anything you put your mind to is possible.

As much as my mother loved her renovated home, the reality was, we needed to consider renting that house out or selling it. The stairs were the deciding factor. E.P.T. needed a single level, handicapped–accessible living space.

Looking at properties was not part of my original plan, nor was it fun. In fact, it was rather painful. For one, my mother was set in her ways and stubborn. Change was not something she was willing to embrace. I endured a lot of pouting and "mother-knows- best" lectures. The East side of Providence was too expensive. We traipsed through property after property. Yet, Esther P. Tunstall always found something wrong with them as an excuse to stay put.

Talk about the eleventh Hour, I finally came across a 55-year-and-older community; Leisure Village! It has all the bells and whistles. One level was handicapped accessible with lots of storage space for all her must have knick-knacks. It was a place where I knew she would be safe, and it was maintenance free. Located in Coventry, Rhode Island, some of her friends complained it was too far for frequent visits. However, my mother assured me that wouldn't be a problem.

The twinkle of excitement in her eyes made me happy to go ahead and secretly purchase this new home for her.

I met with the Owner. We were both straight shooters. We negotiated a price, one that I felt was too good to be true. Before he could change his mind, I went straight to the Bank, got a cashier's check, and solidified the deal. Mission Accomplished! I couldn't wait to surprise my mother.

I think my heart was racing just as fast as the 90 miles an hour I was driving on the highway. I tried hard to keep my composure. My face was flushed with excitement and an energy that I couldn't control. On my way to pick her up, I was trying to think of a way to surprise her. A simple drive up to the house wasn't good enough for me. I admit that I love drama and I was looking forward to seeing the shock and awe on Esther's face. The excitement got the best of me. When I finally arrived at her doorstep and got my mother into the car, I handed her a bag and told her to reach down into the bag to find a surprise. Well, Esther P. Tunstall was not having any of my shenanigans. Never wanting to follow a command without question, or to be the brunt of some unexpected joke, my mother challenged me.

"What's in the bag?" she demanded an answer.

"Just reach in there," I said with a full smile on my face.

"What are you up to?" she queried, not making a move towards the bag.

This went on for several minutes. to the point where I was beginning to be annoyed. Finally, with my patience wearing thin, she pulled the house keys out of the bag.

"What are these keys for?" she questioned me with her frown prominent.

told her it was the house she liked at Leisure Village. All I can say is, next time I'll be mindful how I surprise an elderly person! My mother could have had a heart attack. That's how thrilled she was. Pure joy was written all over her face and that made my heart sing.

I told her she had no house note. It's all yours, paid in full. But there was one stipulation. I insisted nothing could come into this house but her clothes and her knick-knacks. I'd taken the opportunity to buy her a new living room and dining room set. Both were long overdue. She deserved this moment, for all her years of love and care given to me and my brother. For all the losses, pain and sacrifices she endured raising her boys alone. Now, with the additional loss of my stepfather she would be alone, and I wanted her to be comfortable. It was obvious my sincere and loving speech touched her soul. Now

I could board that jumbo jet and head back to work and to my California lifestyle.

Unfortunately, when I returned for another season of work on the set of "ER" the mood had shifted. There was a chill emanating from the crew members. The work environment felt strained.

At first, I was baffled by the 'shade.' This icy-cold attitude from both my crew and superiors cut deeply. Yes, I had taken some time off for personal family reasons, but it was an emergency. Couldn't they see that? I quickly learned it was not just my emergency hiatus. There was a movement in the studios that was fueled by allegations of sexual harassment. Everyone was on edge, including me, because as the only black man on the team, I quickly became a bullseye for their target practice. People can say and do all manner of things when they decide to malign you. More than once, my white co-workers made comments about how I was looking at so-and-so's butt. It was untrue and made me angry. Clearly, they wanted me gone. I had spent four successful seasons on "ER" and enjoyed my job immensely. All the other hair stylists had been fired after a single season. As their Department Head, I strived to set a perfect example of professionalism.

The artic coldness on my job wasn't the only challenge. My love interest, the mother of my youngest son, began expressing unhappiness. I cared deeply for my family. I loved being a dad and had even adopted her beautiful little daughter as my own child. Around that stressful time, we separated. She took the children and moved to Arizona.

Before my girlfriend left, we had seen a judge who ordered split visitation rights. I would see my son every other weekend and 3 days a week. Of course, that was not working because of the distance between ourStates. So, the judge changed the ruling to every other weekend. Well, I could afford to fly to Arizona, so it was no problem for me. But themother of my children could not afford to fly back and forth. Consequently, she was driving. My son would get out of school Friday, and she would get off work on a Friday evening, then hit the highway. They would not get to LA until ten-thirty or eleven at night. I would see himquite late on Friday night. Then, I would have him all day Saturday. On Sunday, we would go to church and then she would call me and say she had to head back to Arizona so he could be there for school on Mondaymorning. I was worried, because I realized something could happen to them on the road, coming or going. It concerned me that a single mom was driving with two children, just so I could be in their lives. The commute was crazy.

Back at my job, the powers-that-be were constantly questioning my capabilities and challenging my credentials and leadership. This went on for months. Finally, I was so disgusted, I couldn't take the humiliation and cold-shoulder treatment any longer. I was pushed to the point of detonation. There was no more fight left in me. It was easier to shut down. I knew I needed to make an immediate change in my life, to save my life. Simultaneously, I was going through all this personal drama in my career and in my personal relationship. My goal was to be in my son's life and to have peace in my world. So, I packed up all my stuff and moved to Arizona.

Upon my transition, the shock was immediate. In the interim of taking my hair license exam for the State of Arizona, I had to find a job. I was fortunate enough to quickly land a Management position at Ultra Hair Salon. I was already well-versed in the drill of hard work and building a clientele. My skill set and experience in styling diverse hair helped me build a strong foundation. My work ethic and craft mastery helped expedite my first goal. In less than a year, I opened my new hair salon. Thus, the "Hair Lounge" was born.

The educational side of my craft has always interested me. I love teaching and bringing my experience and knowledge to those who are committed to working in this trade. When presented with the available opportunity to become a Learning Leader at the prestigious Paul Mitchell school in Phoenix, Arizona, I jumped at the chance. My life was back on track!

In my new community, I had business success, enjoyed the fruits of my labor, purchased my dream home, and established fresh roots. Fortunately, I was able to bless and support my family, both financially and with my physical presence. In Arizona, I re-established a sense of balance and purpose in all areas of my life. The move gave me a renewed appreciation of my career and restored my faith and focus. My California dream had taught me not to take anything for granted and like Bernard Ighner once sang, "Everything Must Change." Finally, all is well with my soul.

CHAPTER THIRTEEN
"Yet Again"

Just when I thought I was on my way to achieving great success, thriving in my new environment, yet again my life took an unexpected turn. My Mother became extremely ill and needed me. As I packed, I quickly realized, uprooting myself to Rhode Island was going to undoubtedly strain my finances. How could I deal with the uncertainty of trying to run my business remotely? It would not work. I had to make an abrupt decision to close my Salon, since I knew I would be in Rhode Island for an uncertain amount of time.

I took the long, tentative drive across country and made it back to Rhode Island in less than two days. I stopped from time to time, to gas up, eat and refresh. But if I'm honest, most of the time, I was pulling over to the side of the road to have a good cry. I was crying for my mother, as well as crying for myself and my uncertain destiny. I calmed myself down by praying to God for the strength I needed to take care of Esther P. Tunstall and I prayed for comfort and peace of mind in my own life.

In some weird way, I felt like a failure going back to Rhode Island. My star-studded life in California had evaporated like ocean fog. My life in Phoenix, Arizona was 'on hold' as was my once lucrative career. There was a sadness in me as I drove down the highway. Wrapping my hands solidly around the steering wheel, I had lots of time to reflect on my life. It rolled before me, like the splash of asphalt pavement.

Where had the time gone? I had moved away from Rhode Island 36-years prior and since then, so many amazing things had occurred to compliment my world. I accomplished dreams and goals, with my family cheering me on and applauding my successes. They knew little about my challenges and disappointments. I kept those close to my chest. Protectively, I always presented a solid picture of success to my mother, my aunt, and my brother. E.P.T. probably thought I was a millionaire.

As I drove, my mind wrestled with emotions and demons from the past. I tried to drown out the voices in my head that threatened to weaken me and destroy my resolve. I knew I needed to be present and positive for my mother's sake. As I pushed the pedal to the metal, I concentrated on my string of accomplishments. In the early years of two thousand, I was busy as a key hairstylist on thirteen episodes of the television series, "City of Angels." I also was

Department Head on the film, "The Brothers" in 2001. It featured Morris Chestnut, D.L. Hughley, Bill Bellamy and Shermar Moore. In 2002, I again headed the hairstylist department on "Undisputed." This film starred Wesley Snipes, Peter Falk, Ving Rhames and Michael Rooker. Riding down the highway, I combed through my mind with care, the same way I brushed and shampooed my clients. I thought about my time of being hairstylist for "Dreamgirls" in 2006 and professionally hanging out with some very funny men on the "Last Comic

Standing" television series. Now that I was no longer in Hollywood, I reminded myself of the good times. Times I spent working my magic in the hair departments of those California studios. I pulled on so many indelible memories that still made me laugh out loud. By the time I arrived in Rhode Island, my spirit was a lot more settled. I was prepared to face my mother, with my smile in place and no trace of the trepidation I hid inside.

Although Esther P. Tunstall was a fighter, going in and out of the hospital and rehabilitation centers took a toll on her. As suspected, my mother's health was deteriorating when I arrived in Providence. Still, she and I shared so many sweet moments, loving each other and always finding some way to share laughter and good humor. She listened to me when I scolded her for not following the rules of wellness. E.P.T. stubbornly argued with me when I disciplined her and often tried to act authoritative, determined to sway me to her unhealthy requests. We persevered through it all together. Months went by. It wasn't easy, but I eventually settled into my responsible caretaker role.

Clearly, my new life in Rhode Island demanded an income. My bills were piling up. As usual, I was resourceful. I knew it was going to take a little longer for me to adjust and align a game plan. Not knowing how long I would be caring for my mother, I put my feelers out to all the local, high-end Salons. I was determined to get my foot in the door. An old colleague and friend of mine, a great hairstylist in his own right, Oliver Cary recommended The Norwich Spa at Foxwood Casino. I was hesitant, at first, to consider such a long commute. The casino was a three-hour, round-trip drive and the position would demand several days a week. I thought of many more reasons not to take that job. If I was completely honest with myself, I thought the position was beneath my credentials. My past was speckled with huge opportunities, celebrity events and legendary participation in award winning shows, films, and television programs. Just as quickly as those thoughts came to mind, I was instantly regretful. This current part of my life's journey became a humbling experience, and I embraced a scripture that came to mind.

"You have not, because you ask not."

This was no time to be arrogant. My bank account was dwindling away, and I needed that casino job. I went in for the interview andwas hired on the spot.

Thanks to that flow of necessary income and finding joy in my craft, I eventually found my footing. I was marching up the path to success. By applying time management, I got the care-taking role down to a science and braided it into my work schedule, without feeling overwhelmed.

This came after yet another home renovation that demanded my attention. At least this time, with a little experience on my side, I half-way knew what I was doing. During the winter months, there had been a very heavy snow. The snow accumulated on my mother's roof, and she didn't want to worry me. She never said a word. However, once I got back home, I discovered she was living in the house, in the cold, with a hole in the roof. As soon as I saw the damage, I knew I had to renovate the roof. Also, the inside of her new home had water damage. It was a mess!

So, me and a couple of my old friends got together, without an iota of formal training between us, we started working on the house. I wanted everything repaired before my mother was released from the hospital. Because of growing up with Pop, my grandfather, and doing handyman work, I had a vague idea of how to fix it. When I needed help, we surfed youtube.com videos. A couple of my friends were felons, and they couldn't get jobs. I was happy to hire them to help me. They were strong men and good people. We rebuilt that roof and redid the whole entire inside of the house ourselves.

Upon returning home, I reconnected with old clients and folks who had inspired me from years past. When we got together, I listened to them telling stories about how they always knew I would succeed. They believed that whatever I put my mind to do, I would accomplish. Those friends have no idea how they propped up my tattered spirit. My sense of style and confidence slowly returned. Certain folks in Rhode Island made me feel warmly welcomed. They celebrated my return and their appreciation encouraged me.

Over three decades had passed since my life in Providence and I took a good, long look around. Surprisingly, I realized there wasn't a lot of focus or development in the minority ownership department. The same class and racial disparities existed between black, brown, and white communities. Opportunities seemed few and far between. I began to consider opening a beauty school. Believe it or not, there was not one entirely black-owned beauty school in my hometown.

Unfortunately, there were a lot of barriers preventing me from taking my Brian Andrew Unlimited brand to another level in Rhode Island. Most of the obstacles were politically based. In between caring for me mother, working at the casino and rebuilding a roof, I put together a proposal that I presented to the City Council. That got me an appointment with the mayor. The mayor got me an appointment with the appropriate senators in my district. The senators got me an appointment with the governor and then I got shut down.

The bottom line became, they wanted me to go back to school and get a cosmetology license for Rhode Island, even though I had a current cosmetology license that had been active for over thirty-years. Additionally, I had two instructor licenses. One from the State of California and one in the State of Arizona. Rhode Island was insisting I go back to school and get an Instructor's License valid in the State of Rhode Island. Why would I go back to school to get an instructor's license when I'm already licensed in two other states? They didn't want to recognize my Instructor Licenses or give me any type of reciprocity. The politicians insisted that I had to go back to school. Then, they had another bright idea. At one of our many controversial meetings, they offered me a state job. They suggested I head a barber and cosmetology program at the Rhode Island State Penitentiary. They wouldn't allow me to open my own beauty school, but they would be fine with my taking over prison program at a salary of $40,000 a year.

"Are you kidding me?" I was obviously upset by their offer. *"I was making over a hundred thousand dollars a year before I came back home. Absolutely not! No thank you!"* I told them.

CHAPTER FOURTEEN
"Not Giving Up"

In 2011, I faced one of the hardest, darkest times of my life. I stood trembling at the crossroads. A well of sadness and a depression took over my life. I had always wanted to give back to my birth community. The politicians rained on that parade. My emotions were painfully raw. No light shone at the end of the tunnel. No glimmer of hope. No praise and worship. Sadly, I didn't have it in me to get down on bended knees and pray my way through this time. I was exhausted. Period!

I didn't realize how many balls I had been juggling at one time. Always good at masking my feelings, my life appeared smooth as silk and seamless in the eyes of many. I was very competent at hiding my weak or vulnerable side, since I didn't want to disappoint my family, my friends and all those I had inspired. Although my dream of opening up beauty school was dashed into a million pieces, happily my mother's health was improving. That encouraged me.

Still, day-after-day the enormity of the grind, twisted and turned like a cement mixer. Round and round, I was driving long distance to the casino, putting in a full day's work and then driving back to my mother's home to be loving son and caregiver. I was on the phone, touching bases with the mothers of my children and endeavoring to be a good, long-distance daddy. I finally had to come to grips with the facts. One, the casino did not pay enough for me to sustain my lifestyle. Two, between my children, child support, my ex's, and my mother, Iwas worn threadbare. Once my mother was well enough, I said to E.P.T.,

"Mom, I have to go back to California, to my industry roots and where my connections are, so I can land better jobs and increase my finances."

Always my best cheerleader, of course my mother understood. She was the perfect example of never giving up. Hadn't she been on death's doorstep? Now, she was back to a healthy state, her home was renovated and warm, and she had spent several months with the son she had desperately missed.

I too had changed. I had grown into a new appreciation of my talents and my strengths. During this time away from Arizona and my salon, amid turmoil, I was encouraged to re-evaluate my life. I reflected on my five Emmy nominations, my participation in the Oscar winning team for the *Grinch Who Stole Christmas* and my Screen Actors Guild Award for Hair Design. Suddenly, I realized, this was a time to reach the next level of my career. Just like Esther P. Tunstall, I was not giving up!

CHAPTER FIFTEEN
"Times are Changing"

As my mother's health improved. I was able to focus and redirect my path back to the journey of my dreams. I knew I couldn't stay in Rhode Island and attain the level of success I could reach. With loving support and encouragement from my mother, I was once again motivated and stepped up to the challenge.

Financially, I couldn't afford the move back to California. Like so many Americans, I was living paycheck to paycheck. This was very unlike the lifestyle I was accustomed to living. One night, in a moment of complete anxiety, I posted to my 1900 followers on Facebook a request. I humbled myself and asked if anyone, who could afford it, might possibly contribute in some small way to financially supporting my situation. I had two responses. One was a sweet response from a client who had been sitting in my chair fourteen plus year.

She replied, *"I don't have any finances, but I can pray for you."*

The other was from my long-time friend, Eric, who replied:

"I'm not responding to this. Pick up the phone and call me."

I'm truly, blessed with great friends like Eric and his wife, Deborah. Their generosity was heaven sent. They offered me the opportunity to live in their home, rent-free, until I got back on my feet. Their support, during a time when my self-esteem and finances were hanging by a short thread, was a pivotal turning point in changing my life.

John Silva, my childhood friend since we were twelve years old, was also of tremendous support. I will forever appreciate the long hours of conversations we shared, as he listened to me wrestling with my decision to relocate. Once I heard from Eric, that decision was solidified.

"I'm heading back to California," I confided to my friend John.

A heavy weight had been lifted. A feeling of excitement bolstered me and gave me new hope! God wasn't done with me yet. In fact, he was showing me that I still had more important work to do.

Once back among the palm trees and sunny California climate, within a week I landed a one-day studio assignment. The project was called, "The Vatican Tapes." It was a demonic, scary film where starlet, Olivia Dudley, becomes the focus of an exorcism. Michael Pena was part of the cast, and the horror movie was directed by Mark Neveldine. I had mixed feelings about this assignment. My soul wrestled with the cult movie content because it was against my spiritual beliefs. I remember confiding in my friend, Eric, about this opportunity. I was considering taking a pass.

"I'm also a man of content and character," my friend Eric told me in a very assertive tone.

"This is your first work assignment since your return to California. I believe you will do well and parlay this opportunity to greater things. Trust me. In this case, you must be a beacon of light in a dark place. It will all work together for good. Be open for great things to come your way from this experience," Eric encouraged me to take the gig.

Well, Eric was right. My one-day assignment turned into a two-week job. Although I continued to wrestle with the script content, I focused on being the best I could be and shining a bright light into the darkness of the subject matter. This led to my being offered work on a popular NBC television series called, "Brooklyn Nine-Nine." It boasted a huge ensemble show with several colorful characters and a bunch of special guest stars. The steady cast included Andy Samberg, Andre Braugher, Terry Crews, Melissa Fumero and Joe Lo Truglio. I worked on that show for one season. This was followed by a movie job on "The Perfect Match," featuring Terrence J, Cassie Ventura, Donald Faison, Dascha Polanco and Robert Christopher Riley. Brandy was in that movie too. I was on a roll!

Next came "All the Way," a 2016 television movie based on events that happened when Lyndon B. Johnson was president and it featured Anthony Mackie playing Dr. Martin Luther King, Jr. After that, I was supremely happy to become key hairstylist on a long-running TV series called "The Good Place." I worked on fourteen episodes per season, for three consecutive seasons, working with the popular actors, Ted Danson, Kristen Bell, and William Jackson Harper.

When I stepped back into the glitter-life of Hollywood, the *Me-Too Movement* was raging. Women were standing up for their rights and unified against the pervasive sexual harassment that Hollywood often covered-up. I totally support equal pay for women, and I abhor any type of sexual assault or disrespect towards females. It was 2017 when Alyssa Milano, an American actress, revealed her story of assault by the powerful Hollywood producer, Harvey Weinstein. That opened Pandora's Box, as a stream of other women came flooding forward with their own accusations.

This made the industry begin to take notice of scripts and story content. The *Me-Too Movement*, (against sexual harassment), joined the popular LGBTQ movement (lesbian, gay, bisexual, transgender, queer, or questionable movement) was fueling a social revolution and a demand for equal rights and more opportunities. The dynamics of our industry were drastically changing. These changes demanded much more patienceand tolerance.

I never allowed myself to be jaded by the industry or to lose my passion and love for my profession. However, I had witnessed many of the problems and challenges that Hollywood workers faced as they climbed the zircon-studded ladder to the stars. I kept my head high and concentrated on doing my best. My work countenance and high standards allowed me to gather significant accolades. I pride myself in being one of the best in my profession. However, in my truth telling, it would be careless and disrespectful if I didn't admit that I both witnessed and received sexual innuendos along the way. I too was confronted and challenged by systemic racism. Prejudice is an evil tool. Over the years, that kind of pressure can take its toll. I sympathize with the *Me-Too Movement* and those who have experienced an immeasurable amount of unfairness because of their sex, their sexual orientation, or the color of their skin. I know that behavior is destructive and can cause great emotional distress.

Speaking from personal experience, on many occasions I nearly lost my confidence and/or my self-control, when systemic racism blocked my professional opportunities. I quickly came to understand the words 'token,' 'inclusive minority' and 'under-represented.' These were key words I heard echoed by managers, supervisors, and the Human Resources Department. Deplorably, I also heard the "N" word used far more than one or two times. Despite the revolutionary climate of change, both in the streets and at the studios, some disparities remained the same at my workplace.

Too often I recall the alarm clock going off at 4am, prodding me to prepare for my day. At that time, I was working on the hit show, "VEEP" with Julia Louis-Dreyfus. At first, I had been thrilled to be back at the studio and doing what I love to do. Now, I was waking up to a puddle of tears as I crawled out of bed. My tears had accumulated throughout the night to remind me, I was drowning in sadness. Sad because I had to swallow my anger over the disparity between black and white employees in the entertainment industry. Sad, because no matter how many complaints by African American actors and actresses that hairstylists were not available and specific for them, the studios still did not want to expand hiring of black hair stylists and make-up artists. Sad, because jealous peers could call Human Resources and lie about co-workers, filing untrue accusations and misrepresentations. Sometimes these complaints were racially motivated.

I've always been a very spiritual and a super sensitive person. These inequities cut deeply into my psyche. I prayed, and willed my mind, body, and spirit to align. I bowed my head, asking for the strength I needed to get through yet another day of uncertainty beyond my control.

I've always been an overachiever. My work ethic is impeccable. I remain the first one to arrive in the morning and often, the last to leave at night. I've worked hard my entire life. I've always been a thoughtful thinker and a caring personality. I'm happy to lend a hand when it's needed and people are quick to tell you, I'm a great listener. Under normal conditions, all those characteristics would be admirable. Nevertheless, when you are the token employee, the game rules change. I was the one that had to reshape my mannerisms, dialogue, and demeanor to provide a comfortable navigation for others. Some people just seemed unsure of how to perceive me. As a strong, heterosexual, black man, one who was styling hair, I faced much discrimination on many fronts.

With my multiple achievements and stellar accomplishments, I quickly discovered I was still considered a threat. It was a daily struggle, to not only have my work judged, but to over-compensate when dealing with people who attacked my temperament. A pasted smile on my face became my non-related work ethic. This was so I wouldn't appear to reflect the "angry black man" perception. I was encouraged to dial-back my personality, to appear less threatening. What? I went from the comfort of my own salon, and easy conversation with my clients, to feeling stifled and oppressed, simply because I was a person-of-color. Supervisors reminded me to "stay-in-your-place." You're not looking at that white girl's butt, are you? Is this 2018 I wondered, or1

Many instances I turned the other cheek, so to speak. However, the bottom line is, what is right is right and what is wrong is wrong. At some point, I had to find the courage to take a stance. Eventually, I had to boldly maintain my own dignity. I had reached the boiling point.

know how women in the *Me-Too Movement* feel because I, myself, have endured sexual innuendos. It was both disgraceful and frustrating to have nowhere to turn. Folks may think men are insulated from workplace sexual harassment, but that's not true. Lack of Union support was another rude injustice and huge disappointment. I was facing sexual harassment and systemic racism.

When I filed a racial discrimination lawsuit against a major film company, my union didn't support me. They wanted nothing to do with it. Even though I won the case, I had to sign a Non-Disclosure Agreement. That means I could never talk about what happened or who was involved. We quietly settled out of court. Still, the word got around.

overheard the whispers and some close to me warned that because of my lawsuit, I might experience retribution from the industry. My attorney's assured otherwise, but I had a sinking feeling that I would soon experience the unfortunate betrayal of a company backlash.

Truly, for a long time, I didn't know how to deal with my anguish. Flashbacks for every wrong inflicted still haunt me to this day. The lack of protection in the corporate workplace is astonishing. Thankfully, strict ordinances are being put into place and that's encouraging. People are paying attention. I continue to hope and pray that a fair and just policy of protection will be instituted for every employee across the board.

CHAPTER SIXTEEN
"Facing the Inevitable"

While in New York on business, I received news my mother's health has taken a turn for the worse. I don't recall booking the ticket or hiring a chauffeured car to the airport. My mind was foggy with thoughts and emotions. Although appearing relatively calm, inside I was seething. Sitting in the limousine, I was silently praying that I would get to my mother, hear her voice one last time; hold her hand and say my goodbyes. These were some of the things I thought about, while approaching the finality of my mother's life journey.

As I boarded the plane, I felt confined and restricted in my seat. Sitting in the stillness of vulnerability, I reminisced. My feet wanted to pace the isles on the speeding plane. My hands held each other and trembled together. My voice longed to scream. I did not know how to process these overwhelming moments of uncertainty.

Staring out the window at the clouds, I felt a sense of hopelessness. In all my experiences of flying, all the many times I looked out that small airplane window, I consciously had never pondered the minuteness of life. Now, staring at tiny shapes below, I thought about the lives that inhabited each home. I considered how insignificant humanity is compared to the entire expanse of space and sky.

I forgot to put my phone on airplane mode. A succession of phone alarms awakened me from a fretful sleep. We were making our descent. Before I looked at the first text, I prayed and reminded myself to be strong and brave. The first message I read informed me that my mother had passed away. I didn't need to read another text. I buried my head in my hands as the plane sped towards Providence, Rhode Island.

With a heavy heart and God's grace, I gathered strength from deep within. I could almost hear my mother's voice telling me, *Brian, get to stepping,* because that's what E.P.T would want me to do! After the landing, I gathered my bags from baggage claim and caught a taxi. I wanted to meet those who awaited my arrival with strength and dignity. It was important to me that my mother's 'home-going' be a tribute to a life well lived. All went smoothly and it was a loving ceremony. E.P.T rest in peace! Now, it was time for me to return to Southern California and continue my dream journey.

"For I know the plans I have for you," declares the Lord, "plans to prosper you and not to harm you, plans to give you hope and a future."
Jeremiah 29:11

CHAPTER SEVENTEEN
"OPEN DOORS"

I've had a lot of flexibility to go back and forth to California over the years. My intent was to keep my union status active. It is uncommon for someone to be away from the industry for months at a time, then return to immediately land prominent jobs.

Reflecting on all my hardships and challenges, I have still been blessed. It was wonderful to work on shows like *Brooklyn Nine-Nine*, *The Good Place* and *Veep*. Not to mention, I received my 5th Emmy Nomination for, *Outstanding Hairstyling for a Limited Series*, celebrating my work in *All the Way*, starring Brian Cranston.

This time, returning after the burial of my beloved mother, I was feeling a little fragile. I had lost my best friend and my biggest cheerleader. However, that loss clearly made me recognize that it's the guidance and examples set by our ancestors that help mold us into the productive human beings we become. When I think back to 'Pop,' my maternal grandfather, I remember he taught me so much with wise words and griot-like history; stories passed from his lips to my ears. Recalling Pop brings to mind the racial challenges he and his generation faced. My grandfather was so proud that he had shown the Kansas City Monarch player, Leroy 'Satchel' Paige, some of his signature pitching moves. Both men lived in a time of American history when racism kept them from participating in America's National League baseball games. But it didn't stop these talented men-of-color from playing the sport they loved and excelling at it. When they were denied access and participation in the National Leagues, they quickly formed their own Negro League. That opened the door for Jackie Robinson to walk through and he finally broke the color barrier. One of Satchel Paige's famous quotes is: *"Don't look back. Something might be gaining on you."* As I move forward, I will take that to heart. It made me proud when Satchel Paige was finally inducted into the Baseball Hall of Fame in 1971. His determination and belief in himself finally knocked down the once, racially sealed door. Sad to say, some of those doors are still nailed tightly shut.

When I think of the guidance and friendship that great Hollywood hairstylists like Peggy Shannon, Ronald Smith and Robert Louis Stevenson offered me, it makes me feel anointed and highly favored. I especially applaud the success of Robert Louis Stevenson, who pursued entry into the 706 Union relentlessly. It still took that award-winning, Black-man-stylist three years of preparation and standing strong in the face of racist rules, before he succeeded as a member of the International Alliance of Theatrical Stage Employees Union. Proudly, he opened the door for me. I will always tribute those who came before me and who helped level my playing field.

Once I returned home to Los Angeles, I knew I wanted to be someone who opened doors for others. One way to accomplish this was for me to become Department Head on my projects. That title and stature give me a certain amount of control over the hair department and allows me to implement hiring practices.

Almost immediately, I was offered a position on a brand, new television series called, *Council of Dads*. I was hired as a hairstylist and flown to Georgia, where they were filming. It didn't take long for me to elevate and become Department Head. The buzz was that this show was going to be a hit. The cast and crew were excited. Critics compared the excellent writing and interesting social characters to the award-winning television series, "This Is Us." In February 2020, I wrapped up a 5-month production on *Council of Dads* as the Department Head of Hairstylists. Then to the shock of everyone, the show was cancelled. This was right before the onset of the pandemic. Suddenly, like a house of cards, everything was shutting down. Consequently, I've been on hiatus for months due to the COVID-19 threat.

Adjusting to the world's new normal, the pandemic placed me in a quiet, yet reflective space. It gave me an opportunity to take a deep breath and invite new energy into my universe. I've recharged my perspective on life, and I've had time to review rough and tough lessons learned. I used this quiet time to download an On-line course and I became a certified Life Coach.

My mission forward is to make sure I serve my heavenly father well, expand my Brian Andrew Unlimited brand, and pursue my non-profit organization with the goal of directing and encouraging young men to become the best men they can be. That's where my Life Coaching comes in.

This has been a season of finality for me. First, I lost my mother and then my father also passed. Thankfully, my father and I had settled our differences, become friends, and I was his support system in the final days of his well-lived life. Luke Tunstall II had the opportunity of seeing his youngest son become successful and excel at his chosen profession. That made us both proud. The loss of my loved ones encourages me to taketime with the people that matter and not to sweat the small stuff.

Let me say this, to all who dream to be a beacon of light in the darkness. We stand on the shoulders of those who come before us. We must know and appreciate our history to walk into the future and balance the present. Our ancestors have passed down lessons of survival. From the slave and the slave master, there are things to be learned. As people of color, like it or not, our battle is more than just accruing an education and being academically prepared. We also must be mentally prepared for the racist agenda that permeates many jobs and opportunities our great country has to offer. Most importantly, we must be strong enough to manifest success in our minds. We mustbelieve in ourselves, against all odds.

As an African American man, living in the United States, I agree there are opportunities out there. There are delicious opportunities made available; exquisite opportunities, like a million-dollar feast at the king's table. The food smells good and looks amazing. You are prepared to fill your plate and enjoy the dinner, but then, you must also be prepared to fight for your place at the table. The remnants of outdated thinking and prejudice based on skin tone still exists, whether we like it or not.

Thankfully, I've seen things changing over the years. I have to say, when I take a close look around, people-of-color are not alone. There is prejudice against the LGBTQ community. Although things are changing, that change only comes when constant pressure is applied. Prejudice is like a deep wound in the arm of society. You must apply pressure to keep from bleeding out.

The *Me-Too Movement* has shown us the ugly, underbelly of womanizing and sexual abuses that women have had to endure. These things remain true, despite all our progress and education. There is prejudice when it comes to inequality in pay between men and women. They stand equal in stature and position, but women often remain under-paid.

The idea behind all these injustices, be they economic, racist, or sexist, is to make someone feel lesser than another. We cannot succumb to a position that makes us feel lower than someone else. I understand the battle cry of Jesse Jackson's Project Hope. Their call to action was, *I am somebody.*

I believe I am as prepared and as good as the next man. I am certain that if I believe in my dream; pursue the dream; prepare for the dream; affirm the dream and live the dream, that dream is bound to come true.

I have challenged myself during these uncertain times with positive re-enforcement. To add to my arsenal of accomplishments, as a barber, hairstylist, educator, consultant and now a certified Life Coach, I remain ready to pursue my ever-evolving path. I am fully equipped to embrace my unfolding dream. Coupled with my educational hairstyling sessions and tutorial zoom trainings, endless opportunities present themselves. One thing I know for sure. I will always keep challenging myself and holding myself to the highest standard.

My book is meant to inspire you. My life story, and the stories of those who inspired me, are meant to encourage, and uplift. In the face of all obstacles, I challenge you to always believe in yourself and to never give up on your dreams. Certainly, I have had my ups and downs along my determined journey. Still, I know there is plenty of room for new and innovative hairstylists to break into this lucrative entertainment world of television and film. With the current, new atmosphere of inclusion, there is an ever-growing need for hair stylists who can professionally style all types of hair. I am not alone when I say that Hollywood needs to hire more African American hairstylists.

At the Black America Website, Gabrielle Union, Yvette Nicole Brown, and Natasha Rothwell, all very popular and busy African American actresses, expressed frustration with having to bring their own hair and makeup supplies, because of the lack of preparation for skin tones and hair textures by the provided Hollywood technicians. Academy award-winning actress, Halle Berry, was quite famous for her pixie hairstyle in movies like her 007 debut, "Die Another Day." She has publicly stated that her short haircut was the result of previous, unhappy experiences with the provided Hollywood hair stylists during the 1990s. Here it is, 2021, and some of the same challenges prevail.

Queen Latifah brought the problem to the forefront, stating she had consistently experienced studio hair stylists who did not know how to style or care for black hair. Queen Latifah, speaking as a successful African American actress, reminded Hollywood that we have all different shapes, sizes, colors and textures of hair.[1] You must be able to work with the hair that sits in your chair. Even Actress/comedian, Tiffany

---

[1] https://blackamericaweb.com/2019/10/29/actresses-speak-out-about-lack-of-hollywood-stylists-who-can-work-with-black-hair/

Haddish reported to NBC news that she had walked off a high-budget film shoot because no one was available to style her hair.[2]

Happily, the passionate profession I chose has afforded me a great life. Doors flew open to allow my talents to shine. Now, I strive to influence the young hopefuls in the business of hair, life and living. It's my turn to open doors.

In the midst of it all, let the record show; all things are possible to those who believe!

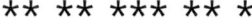

---

[2] https://www.nbcnews.com/news/nbcblk/actresses-cite-lack-hollywood-stylists-who-get-black-hair-n1075761

Walking down memory lane with Brian Andrew and some of the shows and celebrities he had the privilege of working with.

Sammy Davis Jr.
Altovise Davis
Diahann Carroll
Flip Wilson
Marilyn McCoo
Peter Falk
Ruby Dee
Dick Gregory
[illegible]
Adam Jefferies
Jason Weaver
Brandy Norwood
Brendon Jefferson
Erika Alexander
Kim Fields
Kim Coles
Terrence C. Carson
John Henton
Queen Latifah
Mel Jackson
Mark Curry
Holly Robinson Peete
Marquise Wilson
Omar Gooding
Raven Symone
Dawnn Lewis
Nell Carter
Tia Mowry
Tamera Mowry
Jack'ee Harry
Margaret [illegible]
Tim Reid
[illegible]
Avery Brooks
Terry Farrell
Nana Visitor
Rene Auberjonois
Alexander Siddig
Cirroc Lofton
Armin Shimerman
Parminder Nagra

[illegible]
Noah Wyle
Maura Tierney
Mekhi Phifer
Alex Kingston
Vanessa Williams
[illegible] Tucker
Vesta Williams
Della Reese
Kelly [illegible]
Earth Wind & Fire
Deniece Williams
Esther Rolle
Ja'Net DuBois
Brock Peters
Isabel Sanford
Berlinda Tolbert
Marla Gibbs
Danny Glover
[illegible]
Marilyn Gill
Paul Winfield
Telma Hopkins
Ben Vereen
Tanya Hart
Ed McMahon
Louise Fletcher
Bob Newhart
[illegible]
[illegible]
Claudette Robinson
Paul Rodriguez
Billy Dee
Corey Dee Williams
Sheila Johnson
Tina Louise
[illegible]
Danny [illegible]
Tracey Ross
Freddie Washington
[illegible] Varner

Oprah Winfrey
Quincy Jones
Nathan East
Michael Jackson
[illegible]
Little Richard
Mary Wilson
Stevie Wonder
The Temptations
Don King
Will Smith
Martin Lawrence
Olivia Brown
Al Jarreau
Miki Howard
Peter Petrelli
Bill Bellamy
Jennifer Lewis
[illegible]
Eddie Murphy
Natalie Cole
Slick Rick
Tyra Ferrell
The Pointer Sisters
Ed McMahon
Tony Terry
[illegible]
Blair Underwood
[illegible]
Tyra Banks
Loretta Devine
Morris Chestnut
Laurence Fishburne
Stacey Dash
Thandie Newton
Tatyana Ali
[illegible] James
Peter [illegible]
[illegible] Williams
Sheryl Lee Ralph
[illegible] Tiffany [illegible]

[illegible]
Patrice Rushen
[illegible] Smith
[illegible]
Julia Louis Dreyfus
Kristen Bell
Michael Ealy
[illegible]
[illegible]
Andy Garcia
Maya Rudolph
Berry Gordy
Suzanne de Passe
Smokey Robinson
TD Jakes
Mike Tyson
Karen Faye
[illegible] Kennedy
Brooke Shields
Carmen [illegible]
John Mayer
Sonja B. Norwood
Danny Glover
Tichina Arnold
Arsenio Hall & Crew
Jennifer Hudson
John Witherspoon
Rep. Sheila Jackson Lee
Cedric the Entertainer
Troy Evans
[illegible]
Gina Torres
[illegible]
Ted Danson
Sharon [illegible]
[illegible] Howard
Nicholas Ashford
Valerie Ashford
Maya Angelo
Joe Morton
Ernest Thomas

August Richards
[illegible] Anthony
[illegible]
Sarah Wayne Callies
Michael O' Neil
[illegible]
[illegible]
Steven Silver
Hilary Burton
Becky Ann Baker
Clive Standen
[illegible]
Devin Daniels
Rhonda O' Neal
Kimberly [illegible]
Andrea Jackson
[illegible] Demming
Kid n' Play
Eric Griffin
Margaret Colin
Al Sharpton
Jeanne Stafford Cheney
Camille Friend
Louise Anthony
Debbie Allen
Phylicia Rashad
Robert Louis Stevenson
Maynard Matthews
[illegible]
[illegible] Hair & Fashion Crew
Allen Martinez
Shannon [illegible]
[illegible]
Ernest Edward Emmanuel Tunstall
John Silva
Keith Andrew [illegible]
Esther Pauline Tunstall
Lyle Aaron Tunstall Jr.
Lyle Aaron Tunstall III
Elaine Smith
Edward Smith (a.k.a) Ned

Just to Name a few.

The Legends

The Legends

The Legends

The Legends

The Legends

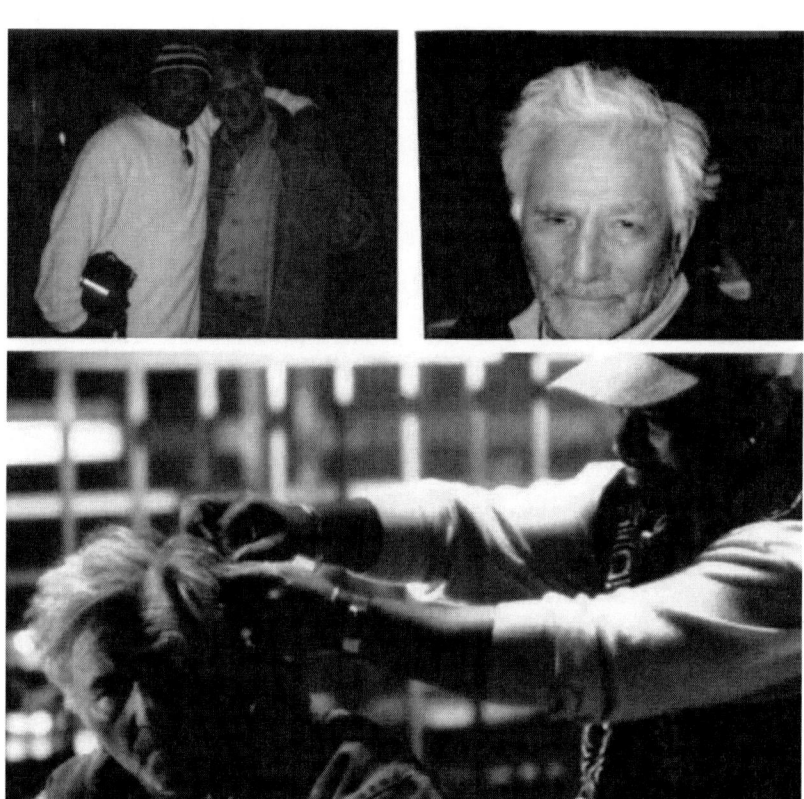

The Legends

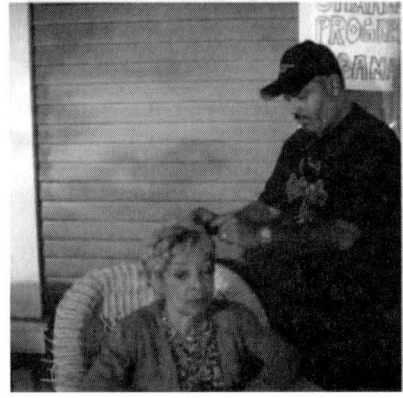

The Legends

"single" stylist

When it comes to keeping women beautiful, Los Angeles stylist Brian Andrew knows a thing or two about the subject. On the *Living Single* set, Brian designs and maintains the manes of stars Kim Fields, Kim Cole and Erika Alexander. In addition, he's styled the heads of Debbie Allen, Marilyn McCoo, Oleta Adams and Tisha Campbell, to name just a few. He's also served as head stylist for Fox-TV's *George* and ABC's *Thea, General Hospital, Prime Time Live* and *Good Morning America*.

When he's not sculpting and cutting the stars' manes, Brian runs his salon, Brian Andrew Unlimited, in Los Angeles. For more on how the hair master keeps the *Living Single* women looking so good, turn to our "Living It Up" feature within this issue.

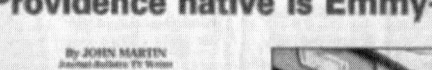

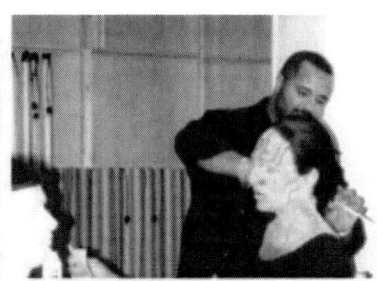

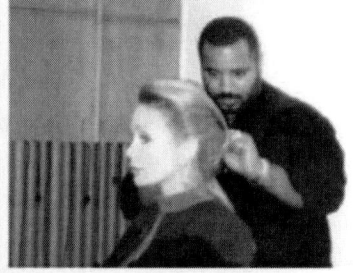
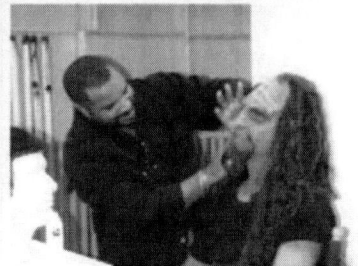

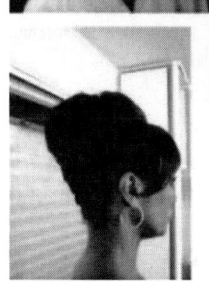

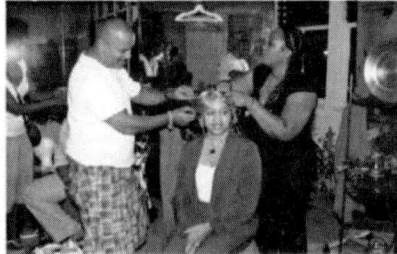

The Journey of a Dream

The Journey of a Dream

The Journey of a Dream

The Journey of a Dream

The Journey of a Dream

Made in United States
North Haven, CT
10 January 2023